CLASSIC COOLING COCKTAILS

SALVATORE CALABRESE

STERLING PUBLISHING CO., INC.
New York

This book is dedicated to my mother,
on the celebration of her 80th birthday.

ACKNOWLEDGEMENTS

I would like to thank my wife, Sue, for her patience; my agent Fiona
Lindsay; Lynn Bryan of The BookMaker, and the bar staff at The
Lanesborough Hotel for their assistance. To my colleagues in the
industry, thanks for the help in sourcing important archive material.

Created by Lynn Bryan, The Bookmaker, London, England
U.S. Editor: Beverly LeBlanc
Designer: Jill Plank
All cocktails photographed by James Duncan

Library of Congress Cataloging-in-Publication-Data Available

First paperback edition published 2003 by Sterling Publishing Co., Inc.
387 Park Avenue South, New York, N.Y. 10016
Originally published in hardcover under the title
Classic Summer Cocktails, text copyright © 2001 by Salvatore Calabrese
Distributed in Canada by Sterling Publishing
%o Canadian Manda Group, One Atlantic Avenue, Suite 105
Toronto, Ontario, Canada M6K 3E7
Distributed in Great Britain by Chrysalis Books
64 Brewery Road, London N7 9NT, England
Distributed in Australia by Capricorn Link (Australia) Pty. Ltd.
P.O. Box 704, Windsor, NSW 2756, Australia
Printed in China

Sterling ISBN 1-4027-0590-5

CONTENTS

■

L'INSTANT
TAITTINGER

INTRODUCTION

■

SUMMER IS A TIME FOR THE EXOTIC AND WITH THE EXOTIC CULTURE COME COCKTAIL FANTASIES. THE CHALLENGE FOR ANY BARTENDER IS TO CONTINUALLY CREATE NEW TASTE SENSATIONS.

On the back of a well-worn photograph in my family album is written: Summer, Hotel Regina, Maiori, Amalfi Coast, Italy, 1968. Look closely and you can see a young boy's head, just above the bar counter. His hands are pouring two glasses of Coca-Cola at the same time. There is a wide smile on his face. He is 13, and dreaming of the sun, of beautiful young girls, sea and sand.

The small boy is me at my first bar job. Without summer, and the tourists that it brought, I would not have developed my love of summer cocktails, nor the skill of the mixologist, the art of entertaining all kinds of people.

Somewhere around the world, it is summer every day, and people are sipping concoctions ranging from a Cosmopolitan and a Cuba Libre, to a Daiquiri or a Piña Colada, or even a Margarita or a Zombie, pleasuring each sip of the sultry cocktails.

Opposite
Champagne and summer cocktails are an essential combination for sweetness and bubbly excitement.

In my first book, *Classic Cocktails*, I compared the bar to a theater, the bartender being a director/actor with a variety of roles. Creating a summer cocktail is like painting on canvas; the bartender is working with color as does a painter. Imagine the background canvas is the glass; the paints are the spirits and the juices, the brushes are the cocktail shaker or the blender, and the juices are the color palette, ready to satisfy your visual sense.

So what's texturally different about a summer mixture? A lot! They use the clear, light spirits as a base. Whiskey, brandy, bourbon, and other darker spirits are put away to the rear of the cocktail cabinet. It's easier to mix a white spirit with juice than a stronger tasting base.

During the Prohibition Era in the United States, Cuba's Havana bars were a dream destination. The bartenders at La Floridita set a standard with their rum-based drinks. Their influence was phenomenal and since then a tropical influence has ruled cocktails, personified in the Piña Colada, with its fruit garnish and that umbrella.

During the '70s the wine bar offered a different style of drinking and the cocktail closed its colorful paper umbrella, packed its maraschino cherry and pineapple garnish in a suitcase, and went home to the sunny Caribbean.

Drink styles changed yet again in the 1980s and '90s, when champagne flowed freely. But it lost its fizz. The cocktail came home and unleashed a cabinetful of combinations of spirits, liqueurs, and juices. I have included a section on bar essentials and a chapter on the blender explains its role

Above
The author, aged 13, behind his first bar on the Amalfi Coast, Italy.

in modern mixology, along with a chapter on the background to summer spirits—gin, vodka, rum, and tequila—and chapters on the Daiquiri and the Margarita. Finally, there are classic and future classic recipes, with a selection of my nonalcoholic recipes.

In *Classic Cocktails*, I found the history of the names of many classic drinks. Now, it is difficult to say definitively who invented some cocktails. Perhaps I could make a plea for our drinks history to be acknowledged and the recipes noted in a database. For in the future, bartenders will want to discover the truth behind some of the new mixes.

So for summer cocktails, my best advice is—be careful not to combine sweet with sweet, nor bitter with bitter.

Enjoy!

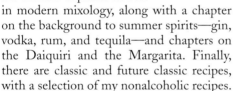

WALTER SLEZAK, FAMOUS ACTOR AND EPICURE, WORKS WONDERS WITH SMIRNOFF.

"HAVE YOU INVENTED A SMIRNOFF DRINK LATELY?"

"Smirnoff Vodka," says Walter Slezak, "is the stepmother of invention." No other liquor has so sparked the creative urge, and led so many people to invent so many drinks. There's a reason, of course. Smooth, flawless Smirnoff has no liquor taste. It loses *itself completely* in almost anything that pours! That's why it's been one continuous triumph . . . from the Moscow Mule to the Screwdriver, the Bloody Mary to the Bullshot. Get busy—and dream up your *own* Smirnoff drink!

the vodka of vodkas

Smirnoff
THE GREATEST NAME IN **VODKA**

80 AND 100 PROOF. DISTILLED FROM GRAIN. STE. PIERRE SMIRNOFF FLS. (DIVISION OF HEUBLEIN), HARTFORD, CONNECTICUT

10

CHAPTER ONE

THE BASIC SUMMER BAR

GENERALLY SPEAKING, SUMMER MEANS MORE FRUIT JUICE, MORE ICE, AND MORE FRESH GARNISHES. AND YOU NEED THE RIGHT BAR EQUIPMENT TO MAKE IT EASY.

THE BLENDER

An electric blender with all the right accessories to make drinks is essential for many of the drinks in this book. Always consult the manufacturer's manual for guidelines. (See page 20 for more information on the blender.)

THE SHAKER

Buy the best-quality brand, since a shaker is for life. Usually, they consist of two metal pieces, and sometimes the top half is made of glass. Try one out for size before buying—you should be able to grip it easily, ready to shake in a vertical direction. The more you practice, the better you will become at the movement.

Opposite

Actor Walter Slezak appeared in this 1958 advertisement for Smirnoff vodka. He made making a cocktail look so easy!

GENERAL TOOLS

bar knife

bar spoon

bottle opener

can opener

corkscrew

cutting board

glass-cleaning cloth

glass jug (punches)

ice bucket

ice scoop

ice tongs

mixing glass

paper napkins

serving tray

spirit measure

stirrers

straws

toothpicks

wooden muddler

GLASSWARE

champagne

cocktail

colada

flute

highball

old-fashioned

goblet

white wine

I prefer fine glasses, with thin lips, sparkling and clear. I spend many hours looking for the right glass to show off a cocktail and it is definitely worthwhile. For a home bar just a few types are essential. A bit of advice: handle any stemmed glassware by the stem, not the bowl.

CONDIMENTS

bitters

coconut cream

fresh chili

fine salt

grenadine

light cream

superfine sugar

Worcestershire
   sauce

12

Garnishes

apples	maraschino cherries
bananas	melon
Cape gooseberry	mixed berry
cucumber	selection
fresh mint	oranges
lemons	pineapple
limes	strawberries

Ice

Ice must be fresh. Use the best filtered water to make it or use bottled spring water. It should only taste of water. Ice is used in the blender and is then thrown away. Fresh, clean ice is used in the glass to insure the spirits are cooled when poured in. It is available crushed, shaved, cracked, or cubed—I use both cubes and crushed ice. Use cubes and cracked ice when shaking a drink; and for special drinks, use crushed or shaved ice. To crush ice: wrap the cubes in a clean cloth, and smash the ice with a rolling pin or a hammer.

TIPS

How to chill a glass

Always chill a glass before you pour any liquid into it. Put the required number of glasses in the fridge or the freezer for an hour before you need them. Or fill glasses with crushed ice before using them.

How to frost a glass

Frosted glasses look fabulous when you present a drink to your guest. To frost a glass, place it in the freezer compartment for about half an hour—less if it is very fine. Or bury it in shaved ice long enough for it to look frosted, and feel ice-cold.

To create a sugar-frost around the rim is simple. Take a chilled glass, moisten the rim with a slice of lemon or lime, and dip the rim in a saucer of powdered sugar.

When making a Margarita, it's essential to have a salty, frosted rim. Rub the rim of a chilled glass with a wedge of lime and dip into a saucer of finely crusted salt. The result will be a superb silvery, crusty rim.

TERMS

Blend

To use an electric blender to make a smooth liquid from a fresh, solid ingredient such as a heavy juice, or coconut cream, or cream.

Build

To pour individual liquid ingredients directly into the glass. Add ice only if specified in the recipe.

Dash
A small amount.

Float
To float a liqueur over another heavier one is simple but you need to be patient. Pour the heaviest liqueur into the glass first, then the lighter liquid over the back of a spoon. This method spreads the lighter liquid over the one beneath it without mixing the two. This method is used mainly in pousse café-style drinks.

Muddle
An ancient term meaning to crush with vigor, muddling is an important part of mixing classic cocktails when using fresh herbs, such as mint. A wooden muddler lets you grind the mint in the bottom of the glass without marking the glassware.

Shake
Always shake for about 10 seconds. If the recipe calls for cream, shake more sharply. Do not shake a fizzy drink. Shake a mixture of egg white, fruit juice, or syrup so it is almost frozen while the ingredients combine in the shaker.

Stir
Drinks combined in a mixing glass need just a couple of quick stirs to combine the

Opposite

Bols liqueurs are based on original herbal recipes and as their fame spread, the company developed other fruit-infused liqueurs.

15

Be a cocktail expert

make your drinks sparkle
with famous *BACARDI*

America's favorite brand · by far

BACARDI COCKTAIL (left)—Sparkle it will—and as a matter of fact, no cocktail *can* be a Bacardi Cocktail without Bacardi Rum, according to good taste, old custom and the N. Y. Supreme Court. Two teaspoons frozen limeade or lemonade concentrate, (or use the juice of ½ fresh lime or lemon with ½ teaspoon of sugar), jigger Bacardi, ½ teaspoon Grenadine. Shake *very* well with ice. **BACARDI 'N COLA** (center)—Pour jigger of Bacardi over ice in tall glass, fill with cola, add squeeze of lemon or lime. **DAIQUIRI** (right)—follow Bacardi Cocktail recipe, omitting the Grenadine. **BE A REAL 100% EXPERT**—Send 10¢ for two delightful food and drink recipe booklets.

© Bacardi Imports, Inc., Dept. 650L, 595 Madison Ave., NY, Rum, 80 Proof

ingredients. A pitcher or jug requires longer—about 15 seconds. If you are adding lemonade or carbonated water to top up a drink, a quick stir is all you need.

Spiral
A thin peel of fruit such as lemon or lime cut in a horizontal direction around the fruit and used either in the drink or as a garnish.

Twist
A thin, long strip of peel twisted in the middle and dropped into the drink.

SUMMER DRINK TERMS
Typical classic summer drinks are those which contain soda water, lemonade, or ginger ale, and fresh fruit juices to make them refreshingly thirst-quenching. There are certain terms for some classic cocktails that are still used today, although the drinks themselves are not necessarily popular. So, here is a guide to the types of drinks you may hear talked about in established cocktail bars.

COLLINS
A Collins is made with plenty of ice. There are two major Collins drinks: Tom Collins and John Collins. Originally made with gin, soda, lemon, and sugar. (See page 94.)

Opposite
Liquor advertisements usually portrayed the art of making cocktails as a simple task anybody could tackle. This 1956 advertisement delivered the message with a broad smile.

COOLER
This is almost identical to a Collins, but contains a spiral of citrus peel that trails over the edge of a tall glass, and any base liquor can be used.

FIZZ
Here is a close cousin of the Collins that is always shaken, and served in a highball glass, with ice and straws. The name suggests an effervescence.

JULEP
This is a long cocktail based on fresh mint steeped in bourbon. The drink's name is believed to be derived from an ancient Arabic word transliterated as *julab*, meaning "rose water."

MOJITO
A term for a drink much like a julep, but the base spirit is rum. Originally created at The Association Cantineros Cuba, the renowned Cuban bar school, it is a very refreshing mix of rum, lime juice, mint and soda water.

PUNCH
In its oldest and simplest form this is rum and water, hot or iced, with sugar to taste and orange or lemon juice for hot and lime juice for cold. Now other spirits and mixers

are added, along with slices of orange and lemon, fresh herbs, and other fruit.

RICKEY
This is an unsweetened cocktail of spirit, lime juice, and soda water that was first made in 1893.

SANGAREE
A 19th-century American mix influenced by the traditional Spanish red-wine-based drink Sangria (Bull's blood). In the early 20th century it acquired soda water. Now it is made with fortified wines, ales, and spirits, and sweetened. Traditionally, spirit-based versions are dusted with nutmeg.

SLING
A term for a spirit-based cocktail with citrus juice and soda water, served in an ice-filled tall highball glass. The word "sling" is an Americanization of the German word *schlingen*, meaning to "swallow quickly."

CHAPTER TWO

THE BLENDER

THERE'S SOMETHING POWERFUL AND SEXY ABOUT A BLENDER SITTING ON A BAR. IT TAKES JUICE, LIQUOR, AND ICE AND MAKES A TANTALIZINGLY SMOOTH DRINK IN JUST A FEW SECONDS.

Sure, a professional bartender could use a muddler but, for some cocktails, the blender does it better. Some bartenders have great panache, turning the cocktail shaker into a blur of metallic silver as hands weave their magic in the air. Whereas the blender is an electric appliance. Noisy.

Probably no kitchen appliance in history has more innovation behind it then the blender. Since 1856, when a patent was issued for a hand-cranked egg beater, more than 1,000 patents have been granted to this device. The next major step in its development was the electric mixer. Many of today's exotic cocktails owe their existence to the blender and, consequently, the specialized drinks blender. The first patent for an electric mixer was issued on November 17, 1885, to Rufus M. Eastman for a mixer, powered by either electric, water, or mechanical means.

Opposite
This is one of the original Waring blenders made to mix fruits and liquids. The basic elements of the design are not that much different today.

In 1904 the U. S. Standard Electrical Works in Wisconsin hired a young farm boy named Chester Beach and a former cashier named L. H. Hamilton. The young Beach improved the first lightweight, high speed "universal" motor, meaning it could run on AC or DC power. In 1910, L.H. Hamilton, Chester Beach, and Fred Osius formed Hamilton Beach Manufacturing Co., by then well known for its kitchen appliance designs.

In 1911, they released the Single Spindle Drinkmixer, an elegant piece of machinery. In 1945 the company released its Triple Spindle Drinkmixer, and even though its design may have changed radically since then, the concept is the same: a motor to drive the spindle, and a glass container for the liquid.

Another major appliance company, Waring, claims it is known for introducing the first domestic blender to consumers. Although the company is named after Fred M. Waring, a popular radio entertainer of the 1930s, '40s and '50s, Waring did not invent the blender, but he did promote it.

Waring history has it that in 1936 Fred Waring had just finished a radio broadcast in New York's Vanderbilt Theater when Fred Osius approached the entertainer with his latest invention. Waring was intrigued with the Osius's concept, and he agreed to back the product, even when the prototype failed to work the first time. Six months and $25,000 later, the prototype still didn't work. And, as you have already read, Osius joined ranks with Hamilton and Beach.

Color-coordinated designs, with metal attachments that magically crushed ice, established the blender as a kitchen essential, and the rest, as they say, is history.

KNOW YOUR BLENDING BASICS

How to get the best out of a recipe? Look at the recipe to determine the order ingredients should be put into the blender. Liquid ingredients should be added first, and can be measured by markings on the goblet's side, or measurement cups.

Fruits can be fresh, fresh frozen, or concentrated. The amount of frozen fruit used will cut down on the amount of ice needed. Fruits that are frozen can be much harder to blend than ice.

Last point to consider: the addition of ice to a blended drink. Not all ice is the same. From shaved ice to hard "pillow-type" ice, each contains a different amount of air and will react differently in a blender. Ice is often measured by the glass the drink will be served in. This gives a good consistency to the drink you are making and takes the guesswork out of how much ice is needed.

CHAPTER THREE

SUMMER SPIRIT BASES

■

PREPARE FOR A NEW STYLE OF DRINK WHEN THE WEATHER WARMS UP. HERE IS A BRIEF GUIDE TO THE FOUR MAIN ALCOHOLIC SPIRITS THAT MAKE THE BEST BASES FOR THE COOLEST COCKTAILS.

GIN

Most of the familiar classic cocktails are made with gin as a base—Martini, Gibson, Gimlet, Gin Fizz, Singapore Sling, White Lady—and for a refreshing drink, there's none better than a G & T (gin and tonic).

You either like gin or you don't. I would rather make a martini with gin than vodka any day. It has more bite, and is more in harmony with the vermouth. When you pour gin, you smell the "nose" immediately, whereas vodka is a little bland.

A BRIEF HISTORY

Gin's past is inexorably linked to the juniper berry and a 14th-century Flemish herbal drink made from its juice. Gin as we

Opposite
It is unusual to find sloe gin requested these days. It still has purist fans who prefer its plum flavor.

FLEISCHMANN'S
**makes America's
most delicious
Gin Drinks**

Right

*Fleischmann's were
one of the earliest
distillers of gin in
the United States.*

know it is a clear aged grain spirit imbued with juniper and other botanical flavors. The drink came to England in 1688, and by the 18th century gin, the people's drink, flowed almost like milk.

Gin was not exported from England until 1850 when excise duties were removed from it. The business expanded when the Americans, who were traveling to Europe, discovered gin cocktails. In 1892 one of the first ready-mixed cocktails was manufactured in Connecticut by drinks firm, Heublein.

The United States Prohibition era caused the British some concern. What would happen to their export market? In the

United States, so-called "bathtub" gin was prevalent but the number of drinkers who died of alcoholic poisoning terrified most people, so they were prepared to pay for imported (illegal) gin. This demand helped to raise gin's prestige and the passion for gin cocktails carried on after Prohibition was repealed in the 1930s.

MAKING AND DISTILLING GIN

The best gin is recognized as that made from a grain, preferably corn, and a spirit with very few impurities. Most gin is made in a continuous still to produce the 96 percent alcohol by volume (abv) ratio required. Once this is achieved, the spirit is then redistilled to produce the final flavor.

The second distillation (for about eight hours) involves the spirit's being distilled along with natural botanicals, including angelica, juniper berries, licorice, orrisroot, cassia bark, cardamon, lemon and orange peel, calamus root, and cinnamon. Which botanicals are in which gin, and in what proportion, is a secret and gives each brand its distinctive flavor. Extra-dry gins usually contain more angelica or licorice; whereas gins with a dominant citrus flavor contain more orange or lemon peel.

The gin is then reduced to bottling strength, 75° proof in the United States and 35 percent abv in Europe.

When buying gin, always read the label and buy only when it states: "distilled gin" or "100% grain spirit". Labels that do not state that are usually full of gin made with flavorings and artificial essences added to molasses spirit.

THE BRANDS

Here is a brief guide to familiar brands that are well established in the marketplace. To list them all would be a book in itself. One to note among the newer brands is Bombay Sapphire with its distinctive shimmering turquoise blue bottle.

BEEFEATER

Founded in 1863 by James Burroughs, a pharmacist who had traveled in America. His ancestors played up the Beefeater image and by the 1960s their brand was the largest exporter of gin to the United States. It is the only gin made in London, and its botanicals are steeped prior to distillation.

GILBEY'S

Walter and Alfred Gilbert set up a distillery in London in 1867. The Prohibition era was a lucrative period for them, to the extent that its label was counterfeited and frosted bottles were designed to counteract this: they were replaced by the original clear bottles in 1975.

GORDON'S

Founded by Alexander Gordon in London in 1769, this company was merged with Tanqueray in 1898 to become Tanqueray, Gordon & Co. Gordon's has distilleries worldwide, and is the second largest-selling brand. Its export brand is 40 percent abv (100º proof), whereas the domestic gin is 37.5 percent abv (75º proof).

GREENALL'S

Thomas Dakin built a distillery in 1761 and the company claims to make gin to the same recipe today. Greenall's Original London Dry Gin contains eight botanicals, and is 42 percent abv (84º proof).

TANQUERAY

The distillery was located near a pure water spa in London in 1830. Its premium brand is America's biggest imported gin, strong at 47 percent abv (94º proof). It was also a favorite of singer Frank Sinatra and the late President John F. Kennedy.

Below
Place your bets on which gin was popular with race-goers!

VODKA

Vodka is a pure spirit, as pure as the driven snow in Russia or Poland, where most of the best vodkas are manufactured. It is as much a part of the northern and eastern European psyche as is life. Now it's a universal drink made infamous by James Bond. All it took was his words in the 1962 movie *Dr. No*—"Vodka martini, shaken not stirred"—and vodka's success was assured.

Vodka is a good neutral spirit to use as a base for summer cocktails, despite its association with a cold climate.

The Russian claim that vodka was first distilled in that country is still disputed. However, the Scandinavians and the Polish can also claim that vodka was made as early, or even earlier.

THE DISTILLATION PROCESS

Distilled from grain or potatoes, vodka's flavor is added after distillation, unlike gin, schnapps, and aquavit. It is also distilled in a continuous still, which produces vodka continuously, not in batches. The key to a good vodka is in the compromise between achieving purity and maintaining the hint of an individual flavor.

The best raw material from which to make vodka is molasses, yet some think this provides sweetness but no positive characteristics. Other raw materials include beets,

Opposite
The Bloody Mary, considered to be one of the most refreshing summer drinks, inspired this 1970s advertisement.

Smirnoff keeps the Bloody Mary on course. Skirmish all you want to over the lemons and the Worcestershire Sauce. Fight the tomato juice versus V-8® Juice battle. But the Smirnoff has to be real Smirnoff for a red-blooded Bloody Mary. Because nothing puts the swash in your buckle like Smirnoff.

Smirnoff Vodka leaves you breathless.

67

31

grain, and potatoes, the latter being loaded with flavors that produce the finest vodkas. The grains include millet, barley, rye, corn, and wheat.

Grain is a local source of starch in Scandinavia and Russia, hence their preference for these two raw materials. Potatoes usually give a sweeter aroma than grain, and rye adds a natural sweetness to the flavor. The differences between flavors are created by the raw material, the quality of water used, plus the methods and techniques during filtration.

RUSSIA

The name "vodka" is the diminutive of *voda*, meaning water. Throughout its development, many additives had been tried, including herbs, spices, and honey, but it wasn't until the end of the 19th century that the ideal vodka was defined.

Major brands available worldwide today include Moscow's Fine Cristall, Smirnoff Black, and Stolichnaya.

POLAND

In Poland, the tradition of distilling strong liquor dates back to the 8th century and it is with feeling that they dispute the Russian claim to be the first. A vodka of sorts, used for medicinal purposes, was made in the 11th century, but it wasn't until the 15th century that it became a social drink. The word in Polish is a diminutive of the word for little water: *woda*.

Bison-grass vodka popular worldwide, features grass from the Bialowieza Forest, where bison have roamed for centuries, eating the local grass.

By 1830 distilleries were being built throughout Poland, many of which now operate under the state-funded Polmos organization, formed in 1973 to control the production of vodka. After 1991 they became independent, although they are still owned by the government.

Leading brands include Chopin, Gold-Wasser, Zytni, Polonaise, Wyborowara, and Zubrowka. Not all of these brands are available worldwide, but they are worth searching for in your local area or when you are traveling.

In a postwar America of 1952 vodka was relaunched with the slogan: "It leaves you breathless." This tag line was inspired by a guest at a cocktail party in New York who, when served a Bloody Mary made with 100° proof Smirnoff, remarked: "Wow. It made me breathless." And it has done that to most vodka drinkers ever since.

SWEDEN

A liquor called *brannwein* reached Scandinavia in the 14th century, and was used mainly for medicinal purposes. Yet by the end of the 16th century it was sold as a drink for the wealthy and by the middle of the 17th century its popularity had trickled down to the masses.

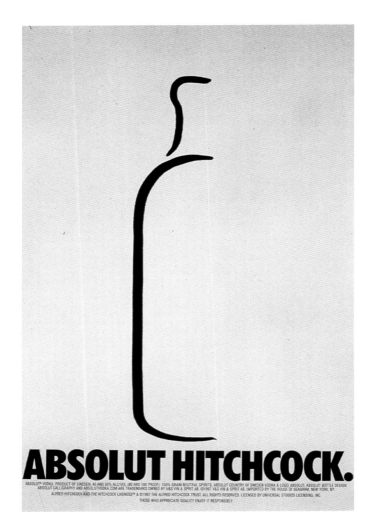

ABSOLUT HITCHCOCK.

After the First World War a government organization called Vin & Spirit controlled the production and sale of alcohol. Crippling taxes and conditions of sale existed until 1955 when constraints were lifted and Sweden's major brand, Absolut, created in 1879 by Lars Olsson Smith, from the small town of Ahus, was revived. He died in 1913, not having made a penny from his creation, which was snapped up by Vin & Spirit, the liquor monopoly. In 1979, the centenary of its production, it was relaunched with a brand new bottle based on an old medicine bottle, using special translucent glass and engraving the label into the glass bottle. The look was successful in reviving the brand's fortunes.

Vodka in the morning flows like cream.

OLD POLISH
SAYING

FINLAND

Finland prides itself on the natural purity of its main brand, made with excellent water. The country has a long distilling history. In the 1600s mercenaries returned from southern Europe with the knowledge of how to produce vodka and it became the national home brew, replacing beer. The main influence, though, came from the Rajamaki Manor factory set up in the 1880s. Just 30 miles from Helsinki, it has access to local pure water. Since 1970 the grain vodka, Finlandia, has been made here for the export market.

Opposite
Sheer genius from the creators of Absolut vodka's advertising.

Right

Two of the processes involved in making Ketel One vodka: (far right) shows the distilling process and (right) the tasting ritual.

SMIRNOFF

Smirnoff is the best-selling vodka in the world. The brand's name has its origins in the Moscow-based Smirnov family. The 1917 Russian Revolution meant the family's factory was confiscated, and the name was entrusted to a family member, but plans to reestablish the name as a successful liquor in Europe failed. In 1934 the North American rights were bought by John Martin, of the (then) relatively small liquor company, Heublein. Americans were slow to appreciate vodka and Martin was starting to rue the day he bought the idea.

Vodka was relaunched in the United States in 1952 with the slogan: "It leaves you breathless." Famous personalities were

approached to appear in advertisements, among them were Vincent Price, Woody Allen, Zsa Zsa Gabor, and the Marx Brothers.

Finally, two newcomers worth a mention. One of the newer brands from France to gain popularity for its purity and finesse is Grey Goose. Another is from Holland. In 1992 the family-operated Nolet Distillery in Schiedam released Ketel One, made in an alembic copper potstill and distilled to appeal to those who appreciate the qualities of a handmade vodka. Companies like the above see the spirit market as being split in two: commercial brands aimed at the mass market, with handmade brands aimed at the connoissuer. There is room for both.

RUM

Aah, rum. The body quivers at the thought of a sip of this sweet and luxurious liquid. The base of many favorite summer cocktails, rum is a Caribbean nectar made from sugarcane, although it is now distilled in other countries.

Sugarcane has been growing abundantly in China and India for 2,000 years and it is thought that a rough type of rum had been made from the molasses even then. Alexander the Great is credited with taking sugarcane back to Egypt and other Mediterranean countries, and it was later introduced to mainland Europe by the Moors, who had learned to distill spirit. Meanwhile, Christopher Columbus took sugarcane plant cuttings to the New World in 1493, which were planted to make sugar. Spanish conquistadors took the skill of distillation to the Caribbean in the 1500s, and the Dutch and the Portuguese set up plantations in Brazil, manufacturing sugar and then producing a spirit from the sweet and thick molasses.

The English, French, and Dutch colonized the eastern Caribbean islands in the mid-1600s and came across a strong rum, made from sugarcane, known as "Kill-Devill," which was drunk by locals. In the 1800s, the British established sugarcane plantations throughout the West Indies.

It was a circuitous route, but to most drink historians, there is no doubt that the Caribbean is the birthplace of rum. It became the main staple of the economy and remains, alongside tourism, an integral part of the economy.

The only sour note in this sweet liquid history is the development of the slave trade. Trading ships left England headed for West Africa, where they traded goods for slaves, then headed off to the islands of the Caribbean. Upon arrival, slaves were exchanged for rum and the ships then returned to England.

Rum was introduced to North America in the mid-1600s and even banned in Connecticut for its bad influence on both the native American Indian populations and British colonists. That did not stop molasses from French Caribbean islands being shipped into New England for distillation and the establishment of a successful liquor industry—until the British government interfered.

A law passed in 1733 heavily taxed the importation of all "molasses, rum, and sugar" from non-British islands in the Caribbean. This Act of Parliament was not popular in the North American colony, and yet rum distillation continued. By then, both the colonials and the local people had developed a taste for it.

When Prohibition was declared in America (from 1920 to 1933), rum smugglers made a fortune bringing drink in from the Bahamas to Chicago, from whence it was widely distributed by the Mob. Wealthier Americans took a flight from Miami to Cuba, which was home to over 1000 refineries. They took (or mailed) home a gift from Bacardi—a postcard showing Uncle Sam, looking a bit giggly, being flown to Cuba by a large Bacardi bat.

HOW RUM IS MADE

Rum is produced from the by-product of the process of manufacturing raw sugar from sugarcane—molasses. When ready to be harvested, the cane stems are full of moist, sweet sap. The stems are then chopped and processed to extract the juice. The resulting acidic, green liquid is heated and clarified and then pumped into evaporators. It is then cool-boiled in a vacuum to produce the syrup from which sugar crystals are extracted. The remaining brown-black liquid is called light molasses; after a second boiling the syrup becomes black treacle, and a third boiling produces blackstrap molasses—a thin, sticky, dark, and bitter mixture containing approximately 55 percent uncrystalized sugar. Other minerals and compounds also remain and this gives rum its aroma and flavor.

The molasses is then turned into alcohol during fermentation when sugar and yeast interact to become alcohol.

DISTILLATION

During this process, water added during fermentation is taken out. Distillation can be done in two ways: via a pot still and column, or by continuous still distillation. The same principle applies: when the wash is heated, the alcohol vaporizes and these fumes are condensed to produce spirit.

AGING

Oak barrels are used to age all rums, be they white or dark. Because wood is porous, it lets the rum spirit breathe, and with each breath, complex oxidation takes place. Oak also gives a spirit tannin, flavor, and color. For rum, a small barrel is best to insure quality.

For white rum, the color acquired by osmosis is taken out during the charcoal filter process, done just before the spirit is bottled.

Light rums are aged for between one and three years. The heavier types (dark rums) are in the barrel for three years or longer, sometimes up to 20 years, and then they start to lose their flavor.

BLENDING

Most rums are blended from a variety of aged rums and different styles of rum. The art of the blender is revealed during this stage when it is his/her decision how much caramel and flavoring and which spices are added. This is the key moment for all brands, when their unique character is set. Once the mixture has "married" (combined well), it is reduced with water to the required bottling strength.

Above
An early still used for making rum. During this process, some rum, like brandy, becomes the "duppy's" share ("duppy" being the Jamaican word for spirit or ghost).

THE BRANDS

This section lists my pick of popular brands that you might like to try.

BACARDI

Bacardi was established by Spanish wine merchant Don Facundo Bacardi y Maso. He had arrived in Santiago de Cuba in 1830 when the island's rum was "raw, dark, and fiery." He saw the future and bought a distillery. By 1862 he had refined the taste of rum, and released his white rum to the world. Its logo is a bat, allegedly suggested by Don Facundo's wife, as it is a symbol of good luck. After the 1960 revolution in Cuba, Bacardi's assets were siezed by the new regime and the family moved its headquarters to Puerto Rico. Among it range of products are Carta Blanca Light-Dry, Carta d'Oro, Añejo, and Bacardi 8.

BUNDABERG

This beauty comes from Queensland, home of Australian sugarcane. Established in 1888 the rum was for locals only until the 1950s when the dark rum was marketed throughout the world. Its logo is a polar bear—odd for a warm-climate rum!

CACIQUE

This rum is from Seagram's Venezuelan distillery and is exported to all major markets. It has three labels; Silver, Añejo, and Añejo 500, a luxury rum to sip neat.

CAPTAIN MORGAN
Three hundred years ago the then governor of Jamaica, Henry Morgan, grew sugarcane on his estate and made rum from molasses. Now owned by Seagram, Captain Morgan is the world's second best-selling rum. Its labels include Black Label, Original Spiced, and Parrot Bay.

CUBANEY
Launched in 1996 in Havana, this rum is sold in the Caribbean, the Canary Islands, Ecuador, Honduras, and mainland Spain. All varieties are made from cane juice: Cristal Reserve; Golden Añejo Reserva (five-year-old); Añejo Reserva (seven-year-old), and Tesoro Dark Rum (10-year-old).

DEMERARA DISTILLERS
Based in Guyana, this South American company is the only producer of Demerara rums. Diamond and Uitvlugt are the two major distilleries where quality control is paramount and their products are sold throughout the world.

HAVANA CLUB
This is the only brand in Cuba, made since 1878, and currently owned by Pernod-

Opposite

Havana Club is the only rum made in Cuba. It is exported to many countries, so buy some and taste the difference from other rums. This 1978 advertisement leaves you in no doubt about its authenticity and versatility.

Ricard in a joint venture with Cubaron. Labels include Silver Dry, Three-Year-Old, Five-Year-Old, 15-Year-Old, and Añejo Reserva.

MYERS'S

Based in Jamaica, Myers's is famous for its almost treacle consistency. It's made from a blend of up to nine rums that have been matured for up to four years in white oak casks. Its Planter's Punch label is the top-selling imported dark rum in America. Recognizing the trend to light rum, Myers's has produced a Platinum White variety.

CATEGORIES OF RUM

I use mainly white and golden rum, with a dash of dark in one of my recipes. Following is a list of the common names used to describe various rums:

White:

Also called silver or light, this rum is clear, light, and dry. Most are not aged, but they are available. White is a great base for cocktails.

Golden:

Also called *oro* or *ambré*, this style is sweet, its color coming from the oak cask or perhaps caramel coloring. Strong in flavor, these can be drunk straight up or on the rocks.

Opposite
*Stills from a
Bacardi past: (Top
left) demijohns
containing the spirit
and (right) the
cooper making
barrels. (Center
left) tasting from
the barrels and
(right) storage
facilities. (Bottom
left) the huge vats
and (right) checking
the bung in the
barrel.*

Dark:
Also called black, this has been aged for a medium to long period in a charred barrel.

Premium Aged/Añejo/Rhum/Vieux:
Mature rums, these are prized by *aficionados*. Best sipped as an after-dinner drink.

Flavored and Spiced:
Finding favor with new rum drinkers, these are usually served with fruit juice or a mixer.

Overproof:
Bottled at 75 percent abv, these white types are in demand for blending.

Single Marks:
These are rare rums from individual distilleries.

And finally,

Cachaça:
Distilled in South America, *aguardiente de caña* is a cane spirit made from molasses, cane juice, or a combination of both. This is the base spirit of a Caipirinha.

TEQUILA

There is no summer without tequila, some say. Without its magical qualities the sunlight is dimmed. Well, they must have had too many Tequila Slammers. Yet there is no doubt that tequila and summer drinks are a marriage made in Mexico, resulting in the Margarita. It used to have a rough and rural image but during the 1990s, tequila found favor with those who enjoy spirits as a neat drink, as well as a mixer with juices.

Tequila is distilled from the fermented juice of the blue agave, a succulent plant found all over Mexico. Spanish conquistadors introduced the art of distillation to the Mexicans and developed the Aztec drink, *pulque*, into tequila. Tequila is a specific *mezcal* (this is the drink with the worm in it, not tequila) and, by law, is made from the blue agave only, and is produced in designated geographic regions, mostly in Jalisco.

The town of Tequila in the Jalisco region was founded by the Ticuila Indian tribe, who had made pulque from the state's blue agave plant since 1530. The town's name means "lava hill" and is probably related to the fact that the town was settled near a dormant volcano.

In 1753 the first distillery, La Antigua Cruz, was set up by Pedro Sanchez de Tagle, producing *mezcal* wine, but a period

Opposite

The humor of South Americans is reflected in this 1990 tequila advertisement.

50

MONUMENTAL MARGARITAS.

CUERVO GOLD MAKES IT.

of Prohibition imposed by the Spanish to protect its wine imports, delayed the opening of more. In 1795 Prohibition was repealed, and Don José Maria Guadalupe Cuervo, a Spaniard, set up a distillery that used cultivated as opposed to wild agave to produce the spirit. This is the origin of the world's leading tequila distillery, José Cuervo.

From that period, through the 19th century it was generally acknowledged that the best *arguardiente de agave*, as it was known, came from the town of Tequila. By the 1870s about 12 distilleries were in business there. During Prohibition in America, enormous volumes of tequila traveled north across the border in an illegal smuggling operation. It was not until 1974, however, that the producers were successful in having a square mile area in Jalisco designated a denomination of origin. In 1976 the whole state was designated. Now, there are 53 distilleries in Mexico, producing up to 350 brands.

How Tequila Is Made

Mature agaves are harvested throughout the year, and its *piña* (the heart of the plant) is taken to the distillery and immediately halved or quartered, ready for cooking, which converts the high starch levels into fermentable sugars. These are extracted from the cooled *piña* by crushing the pulp and washing it with cold water to separate the sugars from the pulp.

The fermentation process takes place in large stainless-steel vats, and most distillers remain secretive about the strain of yeast they introduce at this stage. The actual distillation is a simple process, carried out in pot stills. Tequila is double-distilled, and it is the strength to which it is distilled that creates the character of the spirit.

AGING
The strength, type of barrel, and length of the aging period each have an effect on the resulting tequila. Regulations state that only oak barrels (usually old bourbon barrels) can be used, and the alcohol by volume must remain between 30 to 55 percent.

Tequila, like cognac, whiskey, and other high-end spirits, gains color, aroma, and flavor during aging in wood for between one and three years.

GRADING TEQUILA
Each bottle is graded by the level of agave it contains, as well as the time it has been allowed to age.

Blanco or Silver: the original style, clear and hardly aged. Usually bottled immediately after distillation. Used mostly for mixing with juices or liqueurs.

Tee up with Margarita

Cuervo Tequila Margarita, That Is

Forget that topped drive, that missed putt—with CUERVO TEQUILA... consoling, satisfying. Tequila, favorite of pelota-playing Aztec nobles, today brings delight to cocktail-wise American aficionados. Tequila is pleasurable. CUERVO Tequila is incomparable.

JOSE CUERVO TEQUILA

Gold: this style has the characteristics of an aged tequila, but the golden color is merely an additive such as caramel.

Reposado: the original style developed by Don Julio Gonzales is aged for between two and 11 months in an oak barrel. It is made from both standard and 100 percent agave tequila.

Añejo: produced from 100 percent agave and left for a minimum of one year in the barrel: the finest stay for up to four years.

THE BRANDS
A brief guide to the major producers whose wares are sold throughout the world.

JOSÉ CUERVO
First produced tequila in 1758 from its original distillery in La Rojeña in the town of Tequila. Another distillery, Los Camichines, is located in La Laja in the highlands of Jalisoco. They both produce 100-percent agave tequila for the home and export market. Labels include Blanco, Traditional Blanco, Especial Reposado, 1800 Añejo, and Reserva de la Familia.

GRAN CENTENARIO
Made at Los Camichines, owned by Cuervo. Labels include Plato and Reposado.

HERRADURA

The name means "horseshoe," a sign of good luck in many cultures. It was founded in 1870 and its beautiful historic property contains a museum dedicated to tequila. Labels include Herradura Suave Blanco, Gold Reposado, and Reposado Antiguo, aged for 11 months, Seleccion Suprema Añejo, and El Jimador Reposado.

SAUZA

Don Cenobio Sauza set up the La Perseverancia distillery in 1873 and the company has been a major player in the industry. Its logo is a rooster, symbolizing pride in quality and presentation. It was the first company to set up an experimental agave farm which is still involved in research today. Labels include Blanco, Hornitos Reposado, Galardon Gran Reposado, and Triada (aged 14 months).

Opposite
Tequila was promoted in much the same way as Smirnoff vodka, through the use of endorsements by well-known personalities.

CHAPTER FOUR

THE DAIQUIRI

■

SUMMER WOULD NOT BE COMPLETE WITHOUT A SIP OF A DAIQUIRI, PREFERABLY TAKEN WHILE LAZING ON A BEACH. AT OVER 70 YEARS OLD, THIS CLASSIC IS STILL THE COOLEST COCKTAIL AROUND.

I recently visited La Floridita (*La Cuna Del Daiquiri*), the renowned Havana bar where Ernest Hemingway drank many a Daiquiri made by Constante Ribailagua—El Ray de los Coteleros, (*King of Cocktails*), who reigned there from 1912 until 1952. The Prohibition in the United States had driven mainlanders in search of a strong drink to Cuba. What they found at La Floridita was a perfectionist, a man who could shake liquid dreams from rum and fresh lime juice. Credited as the creator of a number of cocktails, including the Frozen Daiquiri (1927), Ribailagua was a genius.

At La Floridita, the long mahogany counter gleamed just as it must have in the 1930s when it resounded with the sound of shakers full of rum and lime juice. But it was the noise of whirring electric blenders, not the quieter sound of shakers, that filled the bar. I asked one of the bartenders, who

Opposite
Cuba was the place to be seen drinking and carousing during the 1930s. This advertisement dates from 1936.

had been there 41 years, for a Daiquiri and he served me one made in the blender. I was surprised that the bar now makes the Frozen Daiquiri in blenders lined up behind the bar and not in the cocktail shaker filled with crushed ice, which is how it was originally made.

I asked him to make me one the way it would have been made in the 1930s, which he did, with a flourish that would have made Ribailagua proud. The one from the blender tasted as if the ice had become one with the alcohol and juices, like a sorbet, whereas in the shaker-made cocktail I could really taste the fresh lime and rum.

One cannot write about the Daiquiri without mentioning Ernest Hemingway, the American writer. Some say you can still hear his voice in the bar whispering in the clink of cocktail glasses; in Havana he is almost a god and certainly an icon. Papa Dobles (Hemingway's nickname at the bar) helped to make the Daiquiri famous not only by sipping an enormous number of them in Constante Ribailagua's bar, but also by referring to them in his writing.

La Floridita bar has, once again, become the chic place to chill out. A grand mural of an 18th-century galleon entering Havana soars to the ceiling behind the bar, and a bust of Hemingway looms large, as does a collection of photographs; the writer with

Gary Cooper; with actor Spencer Tracy, and chatting with the actress Ingrid Bergman.

ITS ORIGINS

The myth concerns American engineer Jennings Cox and the town of Daiquiri in Cuba. In the hot summer of 1896 Cox is said to have run out of his gin supplies and was expecting important company. His local colleagues drank a mixture of rum and lime juice and it was this, with the addition of granulated sugar, that he offered his guests, naming it a Daiquiri after the town.

 The man credited with taking it back to America, a Lucius W. Johnson, had met Cox in Cuba and took the cocktail to the Army & Navy Club in Washington, D .C.: a plaque commemorating this hangs in the club's Daiquiri Lounge.

Below
Those of you who can visit Havana will no doubt make a pilgrimage to La Floridita,where Hemingway spent many happy hours sipping Daiquiris.

DAIQUIRI

Additional fame came to the humble Daiquiri when President John F. Kennedy proclaimed it was his favorite pre-dinner drink.

Pour all the ingredients into a shaker with ice. Shake sharply. Strain into a chilled glass. Garnish with a wedge of lime.

METHOD: shake
GLASS: cocktail

1¾oz/5cl white rum
juice of half a lime
1 teaspoon superfine
   sugar

FROZEN DAIQUIRIS

The blender has reinvented this classic cocktail. You can make a Frozen Daiquiri with any soft fruit that can be liquidized and added for a different flavor.

Tip: whichever fruit you choose, try to find the same flavor in a liqueur.

Opposite
*Frozen Daiquiri (left)
and Daiquiri (right).*

*Why did Constante Ribailagua roll his limes?
The rolling of the lime separates the juice from the pith inside
the lime. Put the lime in hot water for about
30 seconds—this action releases the juice inside.
Then cut with a sharp fruit knife.*

LA FLORIDITA

METHOD: shake
GLASS: large cocktail

1¾oz/5cl Havana
 Club white rum
1 teaspoon superfine
 sugar
dash maraschino
 liqueur
juice of 1 lime

(The Original Frozen Daiquiri)
This is made exactly the same way as
Constante Ribailagua would have made
it. It has the same flavor as a classic
Daiquiri and the only different is he used
crushed ice to give the drink frostbite.

*Put all ingredients into a shaker with crushed
ice. Shake sharply. Strain into a chilled glass
filled with fresh, dry crushed ice: this
instantly freezes the liquid. Garnish with a
wedge of lime. Serve with a short straw.*

Opposite
*Hemingway Special
(left) and Hemingway
Hammer (right).*

ERNEST HEMINGWAY SPECIAL (PAPA HEMINGWAY)

METHOD: shake
GLASS: old-fashioned
 or double martini
 glass

1¾oz/5cl white rum
¾oz/2.5cl grapefruit
 juice
½oz/1cl maraschino
juice of half a lime

Created by Ribailagua for Hemingway,
who preferred it without sugar, and a bit
more rum.

*Put all ingredients into a shaker with crushed
ice. Shake sharply. Strain into a chilled glass
with fresh, dry crushed ice. Garnish with a
wedge of lime. Serve with a straw.*

Raspberry Daiquiri

Method: blend
Glass: large
cocktail

1½oz/4cl white rum
⅔oz/2cl framboises
juice of half a lime
handful of fresh
raspberries

This cocktail has a delicious rich pink color and a sharp, refreshing flavor.

Put all ingredients into a blender. Blend for 10 seconds. Add a scoop of fine dry crushed ice. Blend for 10 seconds more. Pour into a chilled glass. Serve with a short straw.

Juicing Limes

Take one pale green lime and you have a cocktail. You may not know that there are two types of lime fruit: a large, seedless fruit and a smaller lime. Mainly grown in tropical climates, the lime requires a warm summer to ripen well.

Which to use for a cocktail? Since limes are distributed under varying common names in different countries, it is difficult for me to say which is the best type of lime sold in your local market. My advice to insure a juicy lime is to look for the freshest one with a paler green skin—if its rind is dark green, you will get less juice from it.

Just squeezing the fruit by hand is not enough to get the juice out. Use a hand-juicer—it also stops the seeds (if there are any) from escaping into the juice! Always use the juice straight away. Or, freeze it in plastic containers for use at a later date.

Cool off
with a frosty Daiquiri

Opposite
In 1943 rum had a tropical appeal.
Above
A more sophisticated advertisement.

Next time you
make an Old-Fashioned,
try rum instead of whiskey.
You're in for a
great surprise!

OLD
ST. CROIX
(PRONOUNCED SAINT CROY)
BRAND
Imported Rum

SINCE 1838

COPYRIGHT 1944 GENERAL DISTILLERIES CORP.
BOSTON, MASS.... 86 PROOF

CHAPTER FIVE

THE MARGARITA

COME FLY WITH ME TO MARGARITAVILLE AND
TASTE THE MAGIC OF TEQUILA, LIME, AND
COINTREAU. WHO WOULD HAVE THOUGHT
SUCH A COMBINATION WOULD CATCH ON!

Opposite
*Such seductive
advertising imbued
this cocktail with
such mystique that
it is no wonder it
has an enticing
reputation.*

The day that American actress Marjorie
King walked into the Rancho La Gloria
restaurant, owned by Danny Herrera and
located near Tijuana, Mexico, is inscribed
in the brain of all Margarita-lovers
throughout the world. Without Marjorie,
there would be no Margarita (*margarita* is
Mexican for Marjorie). Herrera mixed and
named this cocktail specially for her since
she was allergic to every spirit but tequila.

This is but one of the myths surrounding
the magical Margarita. Other contenders
to the claim include one Doña Bertha,
proprietor of Bertita's Bar in Tasca,
bartender Pancho Morales of Tommy's
Place in Juarez, and Daniel Negrete,
bartender at the Garci Crespo Hotel in
Puebla. We will never know who did it.

You should discover Margarita

MARGARITA COCKTAIL

...uila Margarita: 1½ oz. Cuervo Tequila.
...oz. Triple Sec. 1 oz. fresh lemon juice.
...ke with ice. Serve in a salt-rimmed glass.

...OSE CUERVO TEQUILA

U.S. IMPORTERS/YOUNG'S MARKET CO., LOS ANGELES, CAL.

TEQUILA

JOSE CUERVO

"LA ROJEÑA"
TEQUILA, JAL.

WHITE
OR
GOLD
LABEL
86
PROOF

67

It was not until the 1950s, when tequila became popular outside Mexico, that the Margarita won the palates of American and European cocktail drinkers. A properly mixed Margarita lets the drinker taste the flavor of the tequila.

Opposite
The scintillating classic Margarita.

CLASSIC MARGARITA

To achieve the crusty look, rub a wedge of lime halfway round the rim of the glass and dip this side in fine sea salt.

Put all ingredients into a shaker with ice. Shake sharply. Strain into a chilled cocktail glass. Garnish with a wedge of lime. Serve.

METHOD: shake
GLASS: cocktail

1oz/3cl silver tequila
1oz/3cl fresh lime juice
⅔oz/2cl triple sec (or Cointreau)

CACTUS PEAR MARGARITA

I used to sneak over the wall to pick these fruit. Boy, are they prickly!

Peel and slice the fruit. Put the slices in the shaker, without ice, and muddle. Add a scoop of ice and remaining ingredients. Shake sharply. Strain the liquid from the shaker through a strainer into the glass. Mash the pulp left in the strainer to add the last drops of flavor. Garnish with a wedge of lime.

METHOD: shake
GLASS: cocktail

1½oz/4cl silver tequila
⅔oz/2cl Cointreau
juice of half a lime
1 cactus pear

FROZEN MARGARITA

This requires just as much attention during its preparation as does a classic Margarita. It is made in a blender using fresh fruit, a liqueur the flavor of the fruit, and crushed ice.

PEACH MARGARITA

Blanch the peach and peel. Remove the stone and cut the peach into four pieces and put into the blender. Blend until smooth. Add a scoop of crushed ice. Blend for 10 seconds more. Pour into the glass. Garnish with a wedge of peach. Serve with a straw.

MELON MARGARITA

Put all ingredients into a blender and blend until smooth. Add a scoop of crushed ice and blend for10 seconds more. Pour into the chilled glass. Garnish with a wedge of melon. Serve with a straw.

Opposite
An 1898 poster by Gustave-Henri Jossot created for Cointreau.

METHOD: blend
GLASS: goblet

1½oz/4cl silver tequila
½oz/1.5cl Cointreau
½oz/1.5cl peach
   schnapps
juice of half a lime
1 juicy peach

METHOD: blend
GLASS: goblet

1½oz/4cl tequila
½oz/1.5cl Cointreau
½oz/1.5cl melon
   liqueur
juice of half a lime
a few slices of yellow
   melon

Just say "Pimm's"

and suddenly
it's Summer

CHAPTER SIX

THE RECIPES

■

HERE IS A COLLECTION OF DELICIOUS
COCKTAILS INCLUDING 100 CLASSIC
AND MORE RECENT RECIPES, 10 OF MINE,
AND 15 NONALCHOLIC COCKTAILS.

In this section, the drinks I have created are marked with a ★ for your reference. They are not classics—yet! Also, here are some useful hints for creating the garnishes which, to me, finish the drink.

• Always use the freshest fruit since a droopy stem of mint or a wilting lemon slice will spoil the look.
• Choose a fruit that is either in the drink, or will match the color of the drink.
• Use a sharp small fruit knife. It's good to take pith and any rough edges off a wedge of lime or slice of orange or lemon.
• Work slowly and carefully when trying to create shapes. The finer the spiral of peel is, the prettier the drink will be.
• Fancy garnishes sometimes require step-by-step instructions and I recommend that you refer to a specialist book if you want to make a complicated garnish.

Opposite
A 1970s image of this classic cocktail was created to appeal to a fun, younger market.

James Bond has his first drink of the evening at Fouquet's. It was not a solid drink. One cannot drink seriously in French cafés. Out of doors on a pavement in the sun is no place for vodka or whisky or gin. No, in cafés you have to drink the least offensive of the musical comedy drinks that go with them, and Bond always had the same thing, an Americano.

IAN FLEMING'S NOVEL, *"A VIEW TO A KILL"*

AMERICANO

METHOD: build
GLASS: highball

1⅓oz/3.75cl Campari
1⅓oz/3.75cl sweet
  vermouth
soda water

This is one of the drinks I like to sip before dinner when I return to the Amalfi Coast. It's a refreshing aperitif first been served in 1861 at Gaspare Campari's bar, a chic meeting place frequented by the composer Verdi, Edward VII, and in later years, the writer Ernest Hemingway. Yet it wasn't until Italy became popular with American tourists that it became known as the Americano. They took the recipe home, and legally sipped it throughout Prohibition—as Campari was classified as a medicinal product!

Pour the sweet vermouth, then the Campari into a glass. Garnish with lemon and orange twists.
Soda water is optional—but for summer, it gives the drink its freshness.

74

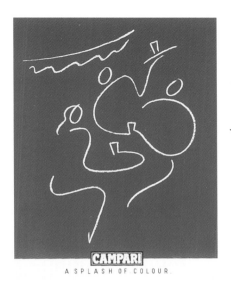

AÑEJO HIGHBALL

Created by Dale DeGroff in his New York bar. I like his way of thinking. Añejo is the Spanish word for old, and in this case, it is applied to rum aged more than six years. This cocktail is his tribute to the great Cuban bartenders who tended both bar and happy souls during the 1920s and '30s. DeGroff has thought carefully about each ingredient and the result is a spicy drink, full of flavor.

Fill a glass with ice cubes. Pour the spirits in first, then the ginger beer, and stir. Garnish with a slice of lime and orange. Serve immediately.

METHOD: build
GLASS: highball

1½oz/4cl añejo rum
½oz/1.5cl orange
  Curaçao
½oz/1.5cl freshly
  squeezed lime juice
2 dashes Angostura
  bitters
4oz/12cl ginger beer

75

AQUAMARINE

METHOD: shake
GLASS: highball

1oz/3cl vodka
⅔oz/2cl peach
  schnapps
⅓oz/1cl Blue Curaçao
⅓oz /1cl Cointreau
3½oz/10cl clear apple
  juice

Aquamarine is the color of playtime, and brings to mind the clear, shallow ocean on a bright summer's day. This shimmering drink has a wonderful flavor through the combination of the apple juice and the bouquet of peach schnapps.

Pour all the ingredients into a shaker with ice. Shake sharply. Strain into a glass with ice. Garnish with a star fruit on the rim. Serve with a straw.

AVALON

METHOD: shake
GLASS: hurricane or
  highball

1½oz/4cl vodka
1cl/⅓oz green banana
  syrup
½oz/1.5cl fresh lemon
  juice
2oz/6cl apple juice
Seven-Up

Opposite
Blue Hawaiian (left) and
Aquamarine (right).

This cocktail conjures up images of the sun and surf in Sydney, Australia—Avalon is one of its beautiful northern beaches. It is an ideal liquid accompaniment to a picnic, providing someone else is driving home!

Pour all the ingredients (except the Seven-Up) into a shaker with ice. Shake sharply. Strain into a glass with ice and fill up with Seven-Up. Stir. Garnish with a thin spiral of cucumber skin (which will twirl around inside the glass) and a cherry. Serve with a straw.

76

BACARDI BARRACUDA

METHOD: shake
GLASS: highball

1½oz/4cl Bacardi gold
⅔oz/2cl Galliano
3½oz/10cl pineapple
   juice
juice of half a lime

Just thinking about the name reminds me of the close encounter I had with a barracuda in the deep, deep blue off the British Virgin Islands. I will never forget it! This drink is not half as dangerous as a face to face with a barracuda... although you may feel brave enough to take one on after a few of these.

Pour all ingredients into a shaker with ice. Shake sharply. Strain into a glass filled with ice. Garnish with a wedge of lime. Serve with a stirrer.

BAHAMA MAMA

METHOD: shake
GLASS: hurricane

1½oz/4cl dark rum
⅔oz/2cl 151° proof
   rum
½oz/1.5cl coconut
   liqueur
½oz/1.5cl coffee liqueur
4oz/12cl pineapple
   juice
⅓oz/1cl lemon juice

My Mama was never quite like this! This drink has strength, sweetness and a delicate coffee flavor, and the lemon gives it a hint of sharpness.

Pour all ingredients, except for the 151° proof rum, into a shaker with ice. Shake sharply. Strain into a glass and gently float the 151° proof rum over the top of the drink. This will give it a strong nose and taste at the first sip. Garnish with a pineapple and a maraschino cherry. Serve with a straw.

BAY BREEZE

A new-style cocktail, it's popular with people who like both vodka and cranberry juice.

Pour all ingredients into a shaker with ice. Shake sharply. Strain in to a glass filled with ice. Garnish with a wedge of lime. Serve with a straw.

METHOD: shake
GLASS: highball

1½oz/4cl vodka
⅔oz/2cl peach schnapps
3½oz/10cl cranberry juice
1¾oz/5cl pineapple juice

BAY OF PASSION

This reminds me of that small and secluded bay on the Amalfi Coast where I used to row vigorously on my way to an assignation...and how I used to row a little slower on the way back.

Pour all ingredients into a shaker with ice. Shake sharply. Strain into a glass with ice. Garnish with a thin slice of orange and a maraschino cherry. Serve with a straw.

METHOD: shake
GLASS: highball

1oz/3cl vodka
1oz/3cl Passoå liqueur
1½oz/4cl pineapple juice
2¾oz/8cl cranberry juice

BELLA TAORMINA

A winning formula created by Fabrizio Musarella, and named after his hometown. This cocktail also looks delicious. It has a spicy juniper flavor, the softness of the Aperol, and the sweetness and aroma of limoncello and mandarin liqueurs.

Pour all ingredients into a shaker with ice. Shake sharply. Strain into a chilled cocktail glass. Garnish with a kumquat cut like a flower and a spiral of lime.

METHOD: shake
GLASS: cocktail

1oz/3cl gin
⅔oz/2cl Aperol
½oz/1.5cl limoncello
½oz/1.5cl mandarin liqueur
⅔oz/2cl freshly squeezed orange juice

Opposite
Bella Taormina.

Above
The traditional Maiori way of carrying lemons from the steep hills to a limoncello distillery.

B E L L I N I

METHOD: build
GLASS: flute

fresh white peach purée
dry sparkling wine
(methode
champenoise)
or champagne

The amazing delicate pink hues of paintings by the great Venetian painter Giovanni Bellini inspired Giuseppi Cipriani, bartender at Harry's Bar in Venice, to create this drink. It is an old Italian tradition to marinade a fresh peach in wine, so Cipriani took it one step further, used champagne and puréed the peach flesh. It was a favorite of Noel Coward and Ernest Hemingway whenever they visited the busy bar. I recommend that you always use fresh white peach purée. When the peach is in season, blanch it to remove the skin, remove the pit, and place the flesh in a blender with a dash of fresh lemon juice. Blend for a few seconds and freeze. As an alternative, squeeze the peach using a manual squeezer and put the flesh and liquid through a strainer to get the best fresh juice.

Quarter-fill a chilled glass with peach purée and fill up with the sparkling wine or champagne. Stir. Garnish with a slice of peach on the rim.

Opposite
Champagne creates elegance and excitement: that's the message in this early advertisement.

BLOODY MARY

METHOD: build
GLASS: highball

1¾oz/5cl vodka
5oz/15cl tomato juice
2 dashes Worcestershire
   sauce
⅔oz/2cl fresh lemon
   juice
pinch of celery salt
1-2 dashes Tabasco
   sauce
black pepper

Harry's New York Bar, Paris, France, was the birthplace of this classic when Fernand Petoit added spice to vodka and tomato juice. The celery stick garnish dates back to the 1960s. Everybody has their favorite recipe. Here's mine.

Pour the tomato and lemon juices over ice in a glass; add the vodka, then spices, and stir. Add a quick twist of black pepper. Garnish with a wedge of lime and add a celery stick. Stir with a stirrer.

BLUE HAWAIIAN

METHOD: blend
GLASS: goblet

1oz/3cl white rum
1oz/3cl Blue Curaçao
2oz/6cl pineapple juice
1oz/3cl coconut cream

This is a classic drink from the original holiday isle of Hawaii in the Pacific, made even more famous by Elvis Presley in the 1970s. This drink will always be associated with his hip-shaking sensuality and enchanting, colorful hula-hula girls!

Pour all ingredients into a blender with a scoop of dry, crushed ice. Blend until smooth. Strain into a glass. Garnish with a slice of fresh pineapple and a maraschino cherry.

BLUE HEAVEN

Maybe created in a slice of heaven Down Under but this tastes good wherever you drink it. Guaranteed to send your tired palate a-knock-knock-knocking on heaven's door.

Pour all ingredients into the shaker with ice. Shake sharply. Strain into a highball glass filled with ice. To garnish, place a maraschino cherry, a wedge of pineapple and a small pineapple leaf on a cocktail stick and place it on the rim.

METHOD: shake
GLASS: highball

1oz/3cl Bacardi white rum
½oz/1.5cl amaretto
½oz/1.5cl Blue Curaçao
½oz/1.5cl fresh lime juice
3½oz/10cl pineapple juice

BLUE LAGOON

A 1960s creation from Andy McElhone, son of Harry of Harry's New York Bar, located in a small Paris street. Designed to show off the color of a new spirit, Blue Curaçao, McElhone served the first Blue Lagoon with fresh lemon juice instead of Seven-Up, which is popular and best for summer.

Pour the Blue Curaçao and the vodka into a glass. Top up with Seven-Up. Garnish with a maraschino cherry and a slice of lemon.

METHOD: build
GLASS: highball

1oz/3cl Blue Curaçao
1oz/3cl vodka
Seven-Up

85

BOLTON COCKTAIL

★ This is a cocktail I created for the American singer Micheal Bolton, who came into the bar and wanted a drink but left it to my imagination, so I had to create something that matched his charming personality—and his expectations.

This is sweet and powerful, like his voice. It has a sharp taste from the raspberries, sweetness from the honey, and power from the vodka.

Pour all ingredients into a shaker with ice. Shake vigorously to dissolve the honey. Strain into a chilled glass. Garnish with a few raspberries in the middle of the drink so when you have drunk it all, the raspberries will be left, soaked with all of the delicious flavors.

METHOD: shake
GLASS: cocktail

1¾oz/5cl vodka
⅓oz/1cl peach schnapps
⅔oz/2cl fresh raspberry purée
⅓oz/1cl lemon juice
1 teaspoon liquid honey

Opposite
Bolton Cocktail.

BREAKFAST MARTINI

METHOD: shake
GLASS: cocktail

1¾oz/5cl Bombay gin
½oz/1.5cl Cointreau
juice of half a lemon
1 teaspoon thin-sliced
   light orange
   marmalade

★ This drink for breakfast? You want to make it through to lunch? It's hot and sunny and you can't be bothered doing much else? Try this—it has a wonderful texture, combined with the spiciness of the juniper, a sweetness and a sharpness. It's refreshing, with a slightly bitter flavor at the finish from the marmalade. You're alert from the very first sip. What a way to start a summer vacation day.

Place all ingredients into a shaker with ice. Shake vigorously to enable the marmalade to combine well. Strain into a chilled glass. Squeeze a thin twist of orange on top (this gives it that extra bouquet of orange) and garnish with a thin spiral of orange.

CAIPIRINHA

Possibly the best-loved Brazilian cocktail, full of lip-smacking flavor. Literally translated, this word means "peasant's drink"—and it has a reputation as the cocktail that could replace the malaria shot! It gets its kick from the cachaça, a Brazilian spirit distilled from sugar cane juice. In the 1920s and '30s car king Henry Ford outlawed the Caipirinha in Fordlandia, his company town located in Brazil. (Not enough concentration on the work at hand.)

Serious bartenders will make this drink with a long wooden pestle, larger than the usual muddler, to bring out the lime flavor, as Brazilians do.

NB: use a medium-sized fresh lime, with a thin skin that's evenly colored. Roll on a cutting board before cutting to aid the extraction of its oils.

Wash the lime and slice off the top and bottom, and cut into small segments from top to bottom. Add the lime slices and the sugar to the glass. Crush the lime to make juice, and muddle to make sure the sugar has dissolved. Add dry ice cubes, the cachaça and stir. Serve with a stirrer, a straw is optional.

METHOD: build
GLASS: old-fashioned

1¾oz/5cl aguadente de cana (cachaça)
1 small fresh lime
1½ teaspoons brown sugar

89

CAPE CODDER

METHOD: build
GLASS: highball

1¾oz/5cl vodka
5oz/15cl cranberry
  juice

A typically American summer drink, named after the Massachussetts coastal vacation area. Sip on the porch before lunch, or as the sun goes down on the hazy horizon.

Pour the cranberry juice over dry ice in the glass, then add the vodka. Stir well. Garnish with a wedge of lime. Serve with a stirrer.

CARIBBEAN BREEZE

METHOD: shake
GLASS: highball

1½oz/4cl dark rum
½oz/1cl banana
  liqueur
2½oz/7cl pineapple
  juice
1¾oz/5cl cranberry.
  juice
½oz/1cl Rose's lime
  cordial

Shooting the breeze out on the deep blue ocean with this long drink is a not-to-be-forgotten experience. Or you could just sit, sip, and be serene.

Pour all ingredients into a shaker filled with ice. Shake. Strain into a glass with crushed ice. Garnish with a slice of lime. Serve with a straw.

CARIBBEAN SUNSET

The best drink to take as you walk along the beach with the girl of your dreams watching the sun go slowly down on the horizon...

Pour all ingredients, except the grenadine, into a shaker with ice. Shake sharply. Strain into a glass filled with ice. Add the grenadine, which will float to the bottom, creating the sunset effect. Garnish with a maraschino cherry set in the middle of a slice of orange.

METHOD: shake
GLASS: goblet

1oz/3cl gin
1oz/3cl banana liqueur
1oz/3cl Blue Curaçao
1oz/3cl lemon juice
1oz/3cl fresh cream
dash of grenadine

CHI CHI

This is a classic cocktail, made in the same way as a Pina Colada—it's for people who don't like rum but like the style of a colada.

Pour all ingredients into the blender with dry, crushed ice and blend until smooth. Strain into a glass. Garnish with a slice of pineapple and a maraschino cherry. Serve with a straw.

METHOD: blend
GLASS: colada

1¾oz/5cl vodka
1oz/3cl coconut cream
4oz/12cl pineapple
    juice

CITRUS RUM COOLER

METHOD: shake
GLASS: highball

1½oz/4cl white rum
⅔oz/2cl triple sec (or Cointreau)
1¾oz/5cl freshly squeezed orange juice
½oz/1.5cl fresh lime juice
few dashes gomme syrup
Seven-Up

A typical tropical-weather drink designed to quench the thirst. A traditional cooler, with a lip-smacking citrus flavor.

Pour ingredients into a shaker with ice. Shake sharply. Strain into a glass filled with ice. Fill up with Seven-Up. Garnish with a wedge of lime wrapped in a spiral of orange peel that trails a little way down the outside of glass. Serve with a straw.

COCOCABANA

METHOD: blend
GLASS: colada

¾oz/2.5cl Midori (melon liqueur)
¾oz/2.5cl Malibu (coconut rum)
3½oz/10cl pineapple juice
1oz/3cl coconut cream

It's hot like the music of the night... a rich combination of rum, coconut, and melon that gives the drink an exotic allure and the color of a tropical leaf.

Place all ingredients into a blender with a scoop of dry, crushed ice and blend until smooth. Pour into a glass. Garnish with a slice of star fruit. Serve with a straw.

Opposite
South Pacific (left) and Cococabana (right).

COLLINS

METHOD: build
GLASS: highball

1¾oz/5cl gin
juice of 1 lemon
1–2 dashes gomme
   syrup
soda water

Usually a summer drink, made with lots of ice in a highball glass.

Here's where the Collins family come into their own. The original Collins cocktail was a John Collins and its origin can be traced back to John Collins, the head waiter at a hotel and coffee house named Limmer's, in London, in around 1790–1817. His original version used a Dutch-style gin, soda, lemon, and sugar. It wasn't until the 1880s that the drink found popularity in America—it was viewed as an upmarket Gin Sling. When a bartender used Old Tom Gin, a London gin with a sweet flavor, the Collins became known as a Tom Collins.

Currently, bartenders serve a Collins made with London Dry Gin, and in the U.S., if you are served a Collins made with bourbon or whiskey, it is a John Collins. Understand?

Add the lemon juice, gomme syrup, and gin to a glass. Top up with soda. Stir. Garnish with a slice of lemon dropped in the drink. Serve with a stirrer.

Opposite
An advertisement for a premixed gin cocktail dating back to the 1950s.

COOL BREEZE

A short drink with a long aftereffect.
It's one of the new wave of Latin-
inspired cocktails to be sipped on a
summer's afternoon.

*Pour all ingredients into a shaker with
ice. Shake sharply. Strain into a glass.
Garnish with a wedge of lime.*

METHOD: shake
GLASS: cocktail

1oz/3cl Midori (melon
    liqueur)
1oz/3cl gold tequila
1oz/3cl cranberry juice

COSMOPOLITAN

My prediction in *Classic Cocktails* that this drink would become a classic has come true.

You can find this drink in just about any quality bar in the world. In the past few years this cocktail has become a star as a new-style Martini. The original recipe used lemon vodka, Cointreau, and cranberry juice. But when it was first served, it had an unimpressive cold color, although the taste was fine. The mystique around this drink is enormous. No one person has laid claim to inventing it—maybe it was the result of a mistake made by someone making a Kamikaze (vodka, lime juice, and Cointreau) adding cranberry juice as an extra. What we do not know is whether the original cocktail used lemon vodka or straight vodka. What we do know, however, is that the original recipe did not use lime juice. Using lime juice binds the ingredients together and gives the drink a more refreshing taste and a wonderful depth of color.

METHOD: shake
GLASS: cocktail

1¾oz/5cl vodka
½oz/1cl Cointreau
½oz/1cl cranberry juice
½oz/1cl fresh lime juice

Pour ingredients into a shaker with ice. Shake sharply. Strain into a glass. Garnish with a wedge of lime.

Opposite
Perini (left) and Cosmopolitan (right).

Cuba Libre

METHOD: build
GLASS: highball

1¾oz/5cl Bacardi white rum
juice of 1 fresh lime
Coca-Cola

Aah, Cuba. Sunshine, sensuality, and a friendly lifestyle. Freedom! The advent of Coca-Cola in 1886 was integral to the creation of this drink. Since in 1893, the myth goes, an Army lieutenant based in Cuba mixed Bacardi rum with the new soft drink, Coca-Cola being the soft drink that the troops brought with them—and proclaimed it Cuba Libre. Literally translated, it means "free Cuba!" The best music to listen to while you sip this lime- and cola-flavored cocktail is by the famous Buena Vista Social Club—pure Cuban sounds.

Pour the lime juice, then the rum into a glass filled with ice. Top up with Coca-Cola. Garnish with a wedge of lime. Serve with a stirrer.

Dark and Stormy

METHOD: build
GLASS: highball

1¾oz/5cl Gossens dark rum
juice of half a lime
ginger beer

From Bermuda, this drink is made with local Gossens dark rum. Simple to make, it's a very refreshing drink.

Pour the rum and lime juice into a glass filled with ice and fill up with ginger beer. Stir. Garnish with a twist of lime.

DREAM COCKTAIL

Here is the essence of all our dreams, combined in one delicious drink. Dubonnet's a classic spirit that's been around for more than a few decades and when combined with the other flavors, it comes to life!

Pour each ingredient, except the champagne, into the mixing glass filled with ice. Stir. Pour into a chilled glass and fill it up with champagne. Stir. Garnish with a quarter of a pink grapefruit slice.

METHOD: mixing glass
GLASS: flute

1oz/3cl Dubonnet
½oz/1.5cl Cointreau
½oz/1.5cl grapefruit
   juice
champagne

EL DIABLO

Literally translated it means "the devil." This may not rank as a classic, but I found it in bartender Charles Schumann's tropical cocktail book and liked it! It turns out the drink doesn't originate in Mexico (as you would think) but in California.

Squeeze the lime juice into a glass half-filled with crushed ice. Add the tequila and crème de cassis. Fill up with ginger ale. Stir. Garnish with a fresh wedge of lime dropped into the drink. Serve with a straw.

METHOD: build
GLASS: highball

1½oz/4cl tequila
⅔oz/2cl crème de cassis
   (blackcurrant liqueur)
juice of half a lime
ginger ale

ELISE

METHOD: shake
GLASS: highball

1½oz/4cl gin
½oz/1.5cl limoncello
½oz/1.5cl peach
   schnapps
2½oz/7cl grapefruit
   juice
2½oz/7cl mango
   juice
⅓oz/1cl Orgeat
   (almond syrup)

One of the winning creations of Peter Dorelli of the American Bar at London's Savoy Hotel, this is a wonderful combination of almond and citrus flavors, the bite of juniper, and the floral nose of the peach schnapps. (He named this stunning drink after his daughter.)

Pour all ingredients into a shaker with ice. Shake sharply. Strain into a glass. Garnish with a Cape gooseberry. Serve with a straw.

GARIBALDI

METHOD: build
GLASS: old-fashioned

1¾oz/5cl Campari
3½oz/10cl freshly
   squeezed orange
   juice

A true classic, simple to make with a delicious flavour from the orange. I love Campari and this combination is simply the best and full of vitamin C! This drink is named after General Garibaldi, the great 19th-century hero who liberated Italy. I prefer two parts orange to one part Campari for the bitterness.

Opposite
Café life: it is essential to sip a Campari as you watched the world go by.

Pour the Campari, then the orange juice, into a glass filled with ice. Stir. Garnish with half a slice of orange.

G I N   R I C K E Y

METHOD: build
GLASS: highball

1¾oz/5cl gin
juice of 1 lime
soda water

The myth surrounding the original Gin Rickey concerns an American lobbyist, Joe Rickey, who, in 1893, liked to drink at Shoemaker's Restaurant in Washington, D.C. The bartender squeezed the juice of a few limes into gin and squirted a soda syphon over the concoction. You can make a Rickey using any spirit as a base; vodka is becoming more popular for this drink.

NB: a Rickey is a close cousin of the Collins and the Fizz—the difference being it has no sugar, and it is made with fresh lime juice.

Pour the gin and lime juice into a glass. Top up with soda water and stir. Garnish with a wedge of lime. Serve immediately.

HARVEY WALLBANGER

There are many myths surrounding this whacky cocktail. This is the one I perpetuate. In the 1960s, a wild surfer named Harvey wiped out in a surf championship and soothed his wounded ego by drinking too much vodka and Galliano at Pancho's Bar, Manhattan Beach, California. Being too full of it, he banged his head against the wall until his friends stopped him. Whatever, the story sticks to this combination of vodka and orange juice.

Pour the vodka and orange juice into a glass. Stir, then gently pour in the Galliano, over the back of a bar spoon. Garnish with a slice of orange. Serve with a stirrer and a straw.

METHOD: build
GLASS: highball

1¾oz/5cl vodka
5oz/15cl fresh orange
    juice
⅔oz/2cl Galliano

HEMINGWAY HAMMER

METHOD: shaker
GLASS: cocktail

⅔oz/2cl vodka
⅔oz/2cl Bacardi white rum
⅓oz/1cl Blue Curaçao
⅓oz/1cl Extra Dry Vermouth
1cl/⅓oz freshly squeezed lime juice

★ This is an unusual combination of a Martini and a Daiquiri. Powerful, sharp and yet a smooth taste experience. A soft, pale blue color, it's reminiscent of the ocean off Cuba. This perfect drink from the Florida Keys is designed to quench even this legendary writer's famous thirst.

Place all ingredients into a shaker with ice. Shake quickly. Strain into a chilled glass. Serve immediately.

HONOLULU JUICER

METHOD: shake
GLASS: colada

1oz/3cl Southern Comfort
⅔oz/2cl golden rum
3½oz/10cl pineapple juice
⅔oz/2cl Rose's lime cordial
juice of half a lime

Freshness personified, with the peach-flavored Southern Comfort providing the sweetness. A perfect drink for any mainlander in need of a bit of comfort down on the beach in Honolulu.

Pour all ingredients into a cocktail shaker with ice. Shake sharply. Strain into a glass filled with dry, crushed ice. Garnish with a slice of fresh pineapple and a maraschino cherry. Serve with a straw.

HURRICANE COOLER

There are many different versions of the Hurricane cocktail, using either passionfruit or blackcurrant syrup. The original Hurricane was a short drink, served in a cocktail glass—a combination of dark and light rums, passionfruit syrup, and lime juice. Since then, there has been a whirlwind of Hurricanes. This one is a delicious combination of fresh fruit flavors ideal for summer.

Pour all ingredients into a shaker with ice. Shake sharply. Strain into a glass filled with crushed ice. Garnish with a slice of pineapple and a cherry. Serve with a straw.

METHOD: shake
GLASS: highball

1½oz/4cl dark rum
⅔oz/2cl white rum
⅔oz/2cl fresh lime juice
1¾oz/5cl passionfruit juice
1oz/3cl pineapple juice
1oz/3cl freshly squeezed orange juice
⅓oz/1cl blackcurrant syrup

105

IMAGINATION

METHOD: shake
GLASS: highball

1½oz/4cl Finlandia
  vodka
1½oz/4cl clear apple
  juice
1 passionfruit
ginger ale

This drink has an apple and ginger flavor, with passionfruit. You don't have to garnish it as the passionfruit pips provide a great visual effect.

Cut the passionfruit in half and scoop out the flesh. Put it in the shaker with dry, crushed ice and add the vodka and apple juice. Shake sharply. Pour into a chilled glass. Fill up with ginger ale. Stir. Serve with a straw.

JOHN DANIELS

METHOD: shaker
GLASS: highball

1½oz/4cl Jack Daniels
⅔oz/2cl Amaretto
⅓oz/1cl freshly
  squeezed lemon juice
ginger ale

★ This was inspired by a line from one of my favorite movies, *Scent of a Woman*. Remember the scene? Al Pacino barks at his young companion that, when he becomes as familiar as he is with Jack Daniels, he can call it John.

Put the Jack Daniels, Amaretto, and lemon juice into a shaker with ice. Shake. Strain into a glass with ice and fill up with ginger ale. Garnish with a thin slice of orange dropped in the drink.

Opposite
John Daniels (left) and Slow-hand Lover (right).

LONG ISLAND ICED TEA

METHOD: build
GLASS: highball

⅓oz/1cl white Bacardi
⅓oz/1cl gin
⅓oz/1cl vodka
⅓oz/1cl tequila
⅓oz/1cl Cointreau
juice of 1 lime
chilled Coca-Cola

This is another classic of which there are many recipes and some premixed versions. Generally, it is made with five white spirits: white rum, vodka, gin, tequila, and Cointreau. This recipe features all five!

Pour all ingredients. except the cola, in a glass. Stir. Top up with chilled cola. Garnish with a wedge of lime. Add a straw and a stirrer and serve.

LOVE IN THE AFTERNOON

METHOD: blend
GLASS: colada

5 strawberries
1oz/3cl dark rum
1oz/3cl fresh orange
   juice
1oz/3cl coconut cream
½oz/1.5cl strawberry
   liqueur
½oz/1.5cl fresh cream

A cocktail with a luscious, languid strawberry flavor that incites you to indulge in great passion on a sultry summer's afternoon.

Place the strawberries in the blender and add the liquids. Add a scoop of dry, crushed ice. Blend for 10 to 15 seconds until smooth. Pour into a glass. Garnish with a strawberry with a mint leaf inserted in its top. Serve with a straw.

MADRAS

A classic that has been usurped by the Sea Breeze in recent years, but it has an interesting, subtle flavor.

Pour each ingredient into a glass, filled with ice. Stir. Drop a wedge of lime into the glass. Serve.

METHOD: build
GLASS: highball

1¾oz/5cl vodka
4oz/12cl cranberry juice
1oz/3cl fresh orange juice

MAIORI MAGIC

★ The Negroni is one of my favorite drinks and here I have tried to create the same balance between flavors.

It is the first thing I ask for when I go back to Maori, and I ask my friend Lello from Bar Pineta to make it for me. I then walk into the garden, sit under a canopy of lemons and reach out and grab one.

Pour the Campari directly into the glass filled with ice. Add the limoncello and lemon juice. Fill it up with tonic. Stir, squeeze a wedge of lime on top and drop it into the drink.

METHOD: build
GLASS: highball

1½oz/4cl Campari
⅔oz/2cl limoncello
⅔oz/2cl lemon juice
tonic water

MAI TAI

METHOD: shake
GLASS: goblet

⅔oz/2cl dark rum
⅔oz/2cl golden rum
⅓oz/1cl triple sec (or
 Cointreau)
1cl/⅓oz Orgeat
 (almond syrup)
juice of 1 lime
2-3 dashes grenadine

The origin of this cocktail is a tale of two bartenders, one being Don Beach at The Beachcomber restaurant in Hollywood, early 1930s; the other being Victor "Trader Vic" Bergeron, 1944, at his interestingly named Emeryville bar, Hinky Dinks. I indulge the Trader Vic story. He mixed a cocktail of 17-year-old dark Jamaican rum, the juice of a fresh lime, a few dashes of orange curaçao, Orgeat (almond liqueur), and rock candy syrup. After vigorously shaking it, he poured it into a glass filled with shaved ice, garnished it with a wedge of lime and a sprig of mint, and presented it to two friends visiting from Tahiti. After a sip or two, they pronounced it to be "Mai tai—Roa Ae," which meant: "Out of this world. The best." Hence the Mai Tai became part of the taste memory of the cocktail cogniscenti.

Pour all ingredients into a shaker with ice. Shake sharply. Strain into a glass. Garnish with either a small orchid or a wedge of lime. Serve with a straw and a stirrer.

Opposite
The Mai Tai in all its delicious glory.

110

THE (NEW) MARTINI

*If God created Man,
then who on earth
created the Martini?*

ANON

Today's new Martini bears little resemblence to the original, simple, and sophisticated cocktail. Always an aspirational drink, imbibed by presidents and megastars such as actor Harrison Ford, the Martini has clearly had a makeover. For one thing it's now mostly made with vodka and an infusion of fruit has been added, making it softer and smoother.

I like to experiment with the new Martini and here are two versions that I think are perfect for summer. Right now, there is a heated dialogue going on in the drinks trade about the new-style Martini. We call these new cocktails a Martini, but are they really Martinis? (Especially when you add chocolate into the equation. Surely this is a chocolatini?) I don't think they are, strictly speaking. These drinks are pure spirit with just a hint of flavor. Only time will tell if any of these new-wave Martinis become classics.

By the way, both of these are shaken, not stirred.

BLUEBERRY MARTINI

Created by Steven Relic at The Lanesborough, London, England. This is a wonderful combination with a superb flavor.

Cut the blueberries in half and place them in the shaker. Quickly muddle the berries. Add the remaining ingredients and fill with ice. Shake vigorously to bombard the blueberry with the ice and release the flavor and color. Strain through a strainer into the chilled glass. The drink will be a perfect shade of blueberry. Spear four or five perfect blueberries on a toothpick and place this across the glass. Serve immediately.

METHOD: shake
GLASS: cocktail

handful of fresh blueberries, rinsed
1¾oz/5cl chilled vodka
½oz/1cl Blue Curaçao
½oz/1cl lemon juice

MELON MARTINI

Put the melon in the bottom of the shaker. Quickly muddle to release the flavor and color. Add the vodka and shake vigorously. Strain through a strainer into a chilled glass. Garnish with small melon balls speared on a toothpick placed across the glass. Serve immediately.

METHOD: shake
GLASS: cocktail

1¾oz/5cl vodka
1 quarter of a small watermelon
dash lemon juice

MARY PICKFORD

METHOD: shake
GLASS: cocktail

1½oz/4cl Bacardi white rum
1½oz/4cl pineapple juice
6 drops of maraschino (cherry liqueur)
1 teaspoon grenadine

A true classic cocktail, immortalized in many recipe books. The cocktail was created in the Hotel Sevilla Bar, Cuba, in the 1920s when the elegant Mary Pickford was at the height of her fame as an actress.

Pour all ingredients into a shaker with ice. Shake sharply. Strain into a chilled glass. Garnish with a single maraschino cherry.

MELON BALL

METHOD: shake
GLASS: highball

1oz/3cl vodka
⅔oz/2cl Midori (melon liqueur)
3½oz/10cl pineapple juice

This is a classic cocktail, and very refreshing in the heat of a summer's day, wherever you are.

Pour all ingredients into a shaker with ice. Shake well. Strain into a glass filled with ice. Garnish with a couple of tiny balls of melon, in different colors if possible, speared on a toothpick on the edge of the glass. Serve with a straw and a stirrer.

Opposite

Bacardi has always made use of the bat image in its advertising. A bat became the company's logo.

114

MIAMI SPICE

★ This is a really exotic combination of spicy rum and fruit juices and one of my recent creations. A sip of this and you'll find yourself in limbo land...

Place all ingredients into a shaker with ice. Shake sharply. Strain into a glass filled with ice. Garnish with a layer of orange slice, a slice of lime, and a maraschino cherry in the middle, all speared on a toothpick across the glass. Serve with a straw.

METHOD: shake
GLASS: goblet

1½oz/4cl Bacardi Spice rum
⅔oz/2cl Cointreau
1½oz/4cl orange juice
1½oz/4cl papaya juice
⅔oz/2cl lime juice

Opposite
Miami Spice.

117

MINT JULEP

METHOD: build
GLASS: old-fashioned

bunch of fresh mint
   leaves
1 teaspoon superfine
   sugar
1¾oz/5cl bourbon
1 tablespoon cold water

The drink's name is believed to be derived from an ancient Arabic word transliterated as *julab*, meaning "rose water." By the 14th century a julep had become a syrup of sugar and water, mainly used as a vehicle for medicine. The bourbon-based cocktail possibly originates from Virginia in America's South. Other states lay claim to its origin, although a 1975 treatise on the subject, written by Richard B. Harwell, states: "Clearly the Mint Julep originated in the northern Virginia tidewater, spread soon to Maryland, and eventually all along the seaboard and even to Kentucky."

It was first mentioned in American literature in 1787 and by about 1800 it had become fully Americanized. It was made with brandy until after the Civil War, when bourbon became more widely available and this combination has remained popular.

In 1803 John Davis, a British tutor working in the grand houses of the Southern plantations, defined a julep as "a dram of spirituous liquor that has mint in it, taken by Virginians in the morning."

Webster's American dictionary refers to a julep as a "kind of liquid medicine." The julep obviously found popularity among Southerners—some 100,000 of them are served each year at the Churchill Downs racetrack during Kentucky Derby Day. The racetrack's Clubhouse started mixing Mint Julep circa 1875—there was a stock of mint out back, and a stock of bourbon inside. The British were introduced to this nectar by sea captain and novelist Frederick Marryatt, who was as enamored with the cocktail as he was with American ladies. The English diarist Samuel Pepys and the poet John Milton also wrote in glowing terms about the refreshing drink.

Purists have been known to mix the mint and sugar the night before a party. But, this gives the sugar time to dominate the mix, not the mint.

Place the mint in the glass. Add the sugar and water. Crush the mint with the back of a bar spoon until the sugar dissolves and the fragrance of the mint is released. Add the bourbon. Fill the glass with dry, crushed ice and stir. Garnish with a sprig of mint. Serve with a straw and a stirrer.

If the mark of a great cocktail is the number of arguments it can provoke and the number of unbreakable rules it generates, the Mint Julep may be America's preeminent classic, edging out the Martini in a photo finish.

WILLIAM GRIMES,
THE NEW YORK
TIMES

MOJITO

METHOD: build
GLASS: highball

1¾oz/5cl white rum
1 teaspoon superfine
    sugar
juice of 1 lime
bunch of fresh mint,
    still on the stalk
dash soda water or
    sparkling mineral
    water

This is a classic Cuban cocktail, revived during the Prohibition era. When I went to Cuba, I visited the Bodeguita del Medio Bar in Havana, famous for its Mojito. It's all they serve. The barman lines up 10 to 15 glasses and it is a neverending parade of Mojitos from dawn until late. The bartender challenged me to make a mojito as fast as he does. And, boy, did I have to work fast. I am fast, but he is really fast. I was playing not on my own ground and the home team supporters were loudest. I have never felt so alone. It was me and a muddler against the world.

NB: the Cuban mint, is not as strong as any of the European mint varieties, and gives the cocktail a more delicate flavor. Use Cuban mint if you can find some.

Opposite
The Mint Julep (left) and
the paler Mojito (right).

Put the sugar and lime juice in the bottom of the glass. Add the mint leaves and muddle. This releases the essence from the mint. Add the rum and fill the glass with dry, crushed ice and fill it up with soda or sparkling water. Stir. Garnish with a small sprig of fresh mint. Serve with a stirrer.

120

MOMA'S PUNCH

METHOD: build
GLASS: goblet/wine

For 12 people

11½oz/35cl golden rum
8¾oz/25cl apricot
  brandy
8¾oz/25cl Passoã
  liqueur
25oz/75cl pineapple
  juice
25oz/75cl freshly
  squeezed pink
  grapefruit juice
juice of 1 lemon
4 teaspoons
  superfine sugar

For garnish
1 orange
8 strawberries, sliced
  through to keep the
  heart shape
half a lemon, thinly
  sliced
fresh mint sprig

★ This is simple to make and has all the tropical essences that you desire in the drink without being too sweet. When you have a party, you want your friends to enjoy a cool, refreshing drink. Also, it will look delicious in a clear glass punchbowl.

Sprinkle the sugar into the base of the punch bowl. Then add each ingredient one by one, starting with the juices and ending with the spirits. Give the mixture a good stir to ensure the sugar is dissolved. Place the bowl in the refrigerator for a couple of hours before your friends arrive. Remove from the fridge and add the orange, strawberries, and thinly sliced lemon. Finally, add a sprig of fresh mint. Add the ice just as the doorbell rings.

Opposite
Moma's Punch.

123

MONZA

METHOD: build
GLASS: old-fashioned

⅔oz/2cl Finlandia
  vodka
⅔oz/2cl crème de cassis
  (blackcurrant liqueur)
2⅔oz/8cl grapefruit
  juice

Before I say anything about the flavor of this drink, let me say I truly love the color. It is purple, the color of kings. The cocktail's appearance is cool and vibrant. It has a bittersweet flavor (like life)—this is a drink fit for royalty!

Pour all ingredients directly in a glass filled with dry, crushed ice. Stir. This will bring out the deep purple color. Serve with a straw.

Opposite
Monza (left) and the stunning Blueberry Martini (right).

MOSCOW MULE

METHOD: build
GLASS: highball

1¾oz/5cl Smirnoff
vodka
juice of half a lime
ginger beer

Herein lies a story of entrepreneurial spirit. This 1940s cocktail was the marketing idea of one John G. Martin, who worked for Heublein & Co., an American distributor of food and spirits. In the 1930s vodka was virtually unknown in the United States and in 1934 Martin bought the American rights to a Russian vodka, Smirnoff. The decision became known in the trade as "Martin's folly," so Martin set out to sell the "new" spirit on the West Coast. While in Hollywood, he dined at the Cock 'n' Bull, then owned by Jack Morgan, who was facing a glut of ginger beer stock. Morgan had a friend who was also experiencing problems; she had to offload copper mugs. The three of them concocted the Moscow Mule, to be sold in a mug stamped with a kicking mule to warn of its kick.

Pour the vodka and lime juice into the glass, fill it up with ginger beer. Garnish with a wedge of lime in the glass. Serve with a stirrer.

Opposite
Woody Allen promoted Smirnoff's Moscow Mule in the early stages of his career in movies.

126

GET A FEW MUGS TOGETHER AND GIVE A SMIRNOFF MULE P

When it comes to entertaining, this is the drink that is. For a cool, refreshing Mule made with Smirnoff and 7-Up® is a delicious treat you can start with and stay with. Only crystal clear Smirnoff, filtered through 14,000 lbs. of activated charcoal, blends so perfectly with the flavor of 7-Up. So never forget the rule for the Mule. Make it with *Smirnoff.*

Smirnoff it leaves you breathless

127

JAMAICAN MULE

METHOD: build
GLASS: highball

¾oz/5cl dark Jamaican
rum
juice of half a lime
ginger beer

An exotic tropical version of the Moscow Mule, made with dark rum.

Pour rum and lime juice into the glass. Top up with ginger beer. Garnish with a wedge of lime in the glass.

PARADISE PUNCH

METHOD: shake
GLASS: highball

1oz/3cl Southern
Comfort
⅔oz/2cl vodka
½oz/1.5cl Amaretto
½oz/1.5cl freshly
squeezed orange
juice
1¾oz/5cl pineapple
juice
⅔oz/2cl Rose's lime
cordial
2 dashes grenadine

If Paradise is half as nice as the state of mind that this cocktail brings on, then lead me to it! A combination of lots of ingredients, full of flavor, that creates a harmonious cocktail.

Pour all ingredients into a shaker with ice. Shake sharply. Strain into a glass filled with ice. Garnish with a slice of lime and a maraschino cherry.

PERINI

This was created by Jerry Mignot. A balanced combination of cranberry juice and fresh blended pear, with champagne adding the sparkle. Pick a ripe pear for a natural sweetness.

To make the pear pureé, peel the pear and remove the core. Put it in a blender with a dash of dry white wine and blend until smooth. Add equal quantities of cranberry juice and pear pureé to the glass. Add a dash of Poire William, the schnapps, and fill with champagne. Stir. Garnish with a slice of pear and a few cranberries on a stem. Serve immediately.

METHOD: build
GLASS: flute

1¾oz/2.5cl cranberry juice
1¾oz/2.5cl fresh pear purée
½oz/1cl pear schnapps (Poire William)
champagne

PIMM'S NO. 1

METHOD: build
GLASS: highball

This recipe is for one. Multiply it by the number of party guests you're expecting.

5cl/1¾oz Pimm's No. 1 cup
Seven-Up or ginger ale
lemon and orange slices
cucumber peel
sprig of fresh mint or borage

Created in 1840 as a digestive tonic by James Pimm and served at his oyster bar in London's financial center, this concoction of herbs and quinine caught on. By the 1920s the Pimm's No. 1 cup was distributed throughout England and exported to the colonies.

Pimm's No. 1 has a secret recipe which is known only to six people. These days, this is the only premixed cocktail used by a professional bartender. There are three flavors in a Pimm's: the dry taste when it's mixed just with soda water; the spicy taste when ginger ale is added, and then the sweeter, classic version made with Seven-Up.

NB: borage, or starflower, an herb that's often used to decorate a glass of Pimm's, has natural healing powers and is currently being used to combat breast cancer.

Opposite
Pimm's was always advertised as a respectable drink that creates a sense of fun among friends.

Pour the Pimm's into a highball glass filled with ice. Top up with Seven-Up or ginger ale. Finally, add the sliced fruit and stir. Garnish with a slice of lemon and orange, the rind of a cucumber and a sprig of fresh mint (or borage) in the glass. Serve with a straw.

PIMM'S ROYALE

For those who like a bit of luxury. Instead of Seven-Up or ginger ale, add champagne or sparkling wine. Add fruit as well for a pleasant surprise.

Pimms makes beginners less bashful
Pimms makes old timers less staid
Pimms adds 'Carramba's' to cha chas and sambas,
Add lemonade and it's made.

PIMMS

The No. 1 PARTY DRINK

Pimms plus fizzy lemonade and ice, topped with a slice of lemon, tastes delicious.

Send for Pimms Party leaflet to : Pimms, 100 Bishopsgate, E.C.2.

PIÑA COLADA

The most infamous of the coladas is the Piña Colada—its title means "strained pineapple." There is a bit of a stigma attached to this drink in the third millenium, yet there are still fans who will drink no other. This drink originated in Puerto Rico and there are two contenders who claim to have invented the recipe. Ramon Marrero Perez of the Caribe Hilton is adamant he mixed the first in 1954; Don Ramon Portas Mingot of La Barrachina Restaurant Bar staked his claim almost a decade later—1963.

Use the freshest fruit you can buy. This cocktail should be smooth and easy to drink and should be milky white, not separated into clear liquid and froth.

Pour the pineapple juice (or the 3 slices of pineapple) into the blender and add the coconut cream and the white rum. Blend for a few seconds. Add the crushed ice and blend for 5 seconds. Pour into a glass. Garnish with a quarter slice of fresh pineapple speared with a maraschino cherry. Or put a star fruit on the rim. Serve with a straw.

METHOD: blend
GLASS: colada/goblet

1¾oz/5cl Bacardi white rum
3½oz/10cl pineapple juice or three slices canned pineapple
1¾oz/5cl coconut cream
crushed ice

Opposite
A classic Piña Colada (left) and Love in the Afternoon (right).

133

Here are three more versions of the fruity colada that I think work well as summer cocktails. The Chocolate Colada is for all of you who love the smooth and creamy taste of chocolate.

APPLE COLADA

METHOD: blend
GLASS: colada

1½oz/4cl white rum
⅔oz/2cl apple schnapps
1oz/3cl coconut cream
2½oz/7cl natural apple juice
half an apple, peeled
half teaspoon superfine sugar

The apple flavor in this cocktail is immediately refreshing. Blending the apple adds an extra texture to the final drink.

Place all ingredients into a blender. Blend for 10 seconds. Add a scoop of crushed ice and blend for 10 seconds more until smooth. Garnish with a wedge of apple cut in 3 fine slices, to which you add a maraschino cherry, and spear all on a toothpick. Serve with a straw.

CHOCO COLADA

Created by Charles Schumann, a renowned cocktail creator and author, who perhaps has a very sweet tooth. But, seriously, this is a deliciously smooth colada for those to whom chocolate is the food of love.

Pour all ingredients into a blender. Blend for 10 seconds. Strain into a glass. Sprinkle with chocolate shavings. Serve with a straw.

METHOD: blend
GLASS: colada/goblet

1½oz/4cl sweet cream
  or milk
⅔oz/2cl chocolate syrup
⅓oz/1cl Tia Maria or
  Kahlua
1½oz/4cl white rum
⅓oz/1cl dark rum
1¾oz/5cl coconut cream

MANGO COLADA

A gorgeous color, fresh and enticing, this is a melt-in-the-mouth drink based on the original recipe.

Place all ingredients into a blender with crushed ice. Blend for 15 seconds until smooth. Pour the mixture into a glass. Garnish with a thin slice of mango on the rim of the glass. Serve with a straw.

METHOD: blend
GLASS: colada/goblet

1¾oz/5cl golden rum
1oz/3cl coconut cream
2½oz/7cl fresh mango
  juice
quarter of a fresh
  mango, sliced

Following pages
A delicious 1984 Piña Colada advertisement.

135

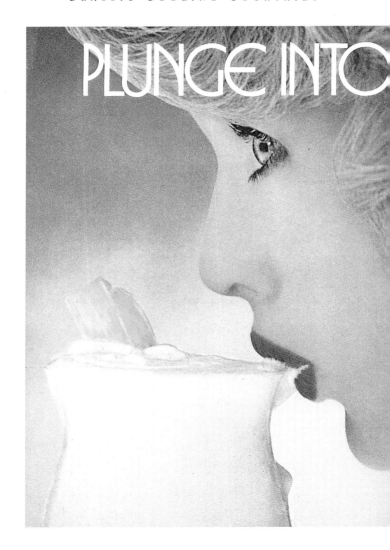

PLUNGE INTO

137

PLANTER'S PUNCH NO.1 (THE ORIGINAL)

METHOD: shake
GLASS:

1¾oz/5cl Myers's dark
   rum
2 dashes gomme syrup
1 dash Angostura
   bitters
juice of half a lemon

Pour all ingredients into a shaker with ice. Shake sharply. Strain into a glass with ice. Garnish with a slice of orange and a maraschino cherry and a sprig of fresh mint. Serve with a straw.

NB: you can add soda water to make it more refreshing.

PLANTER'S PUNCH NO. 2

METHOD: shake
GLASS: highball

⅔oz/2cl Myers's dark
   rum
1oz/3cl white rum
⅓oz/1cl Cointreau
1¾oz/5cl pineapple
   juice
1¾oz/5cl freshly
   squeezed orange
   juice
juice of half a lime
2 dashes grenadine

This is a much more interesting drink, longer and fruitier, full of texture and more flavors. It includes white as well as dark rum, and lime juice, instead of lemon.

Pour all ingredients except the dark rum into a shaker with ice. Shake sharply. Strain into a glass with ice. Carefully float the dark rum on top. Garnish with a slice of orange and a maraschino cherry. Serve with a straw.

R O S S I N I

Music by the great Italian composer must have been playing while the original bartender created this drink: soft and mellow, it's a delicious mixture of sweet strawberry flavor, and a burst of fizz from champagne.

Put the strawberries in a blender, with a splash of wine, and blend until smooth. Pour into a chilled flute and fill it up with champagne. Stir. Garnish with a strawberry.

METHOD: blend/build
GLASS: flute

4 to 6 fresh
   strawberries
champagne
dry white wine

S A L T Y   D O G

I am totally bemused by the variety of recipes for this classic. Some say gin; others say vodka. I prefer vodka. I like the salt and grapefruit combination, producing a slightly bitter flavor.

Rub the rim of the glass with a wedge of lemon. Dip the rim into a saucer of fine salt to make a crusty effect. Pour the vodka and grapefruit juice into a shaker with ice. Shake sharply. Strain into a glass. Serve.

METHOD: shake
GLASS: cocktail

1½oz/4cl vodka
1½oz/4cl fresh
   grapefruit juice

SANGRIA

METHOD: build
GLASS: wine or goblet

Serves 4 people

1 bottle of Spanish red
  wine
4oz/12cl Spanish
  brandy
1oz/3cl triple sec (or
  Cointreau)
soda water (optional)
2 teaspoons superfine
  sugar
juice of half a lemon
juice of half an orange
half an apple, orange,
  lemon, and lime,
  sliced

There are many versions of Sangria, a classic Spanish party drink usually containing the local liqueur. *Sangria* is the Spanish word for "bleeding," and comes from *sangre,* meaning "blood," or "the color of blood." This is drunk at many festivals with theatricality— the art lies in being able to drink the Sangria from varying heights without spilling any. A popular drink, cool and packed with fruit.

You can make and serve it in either a jug or small punch bowl.

Pour all ingredients into the container, beginning with the sugar, adding the brandy, the triple sec (or Cointreau), and the orange and lemon juice, then the wine. Stir to dissolve sugar and leave to marinate in the refrigerator for a couple of hours before serving. When ready to serve, add the lemon, orange, lime, and thin apple slices. If want to be more adventurous, add fresh strawberries, blackberries, or raspberries for a more fruity flavor. I recommend you add slices of hard peaches—they soak up the wine better than soft peaches. Add ice, not too much (so as not to dilute it) and finally, when guests arrive, add soda water, to make it refreshing.

SCORPION

One of the delicious cocktails invented by Victor "Trader Vic" Bergeron in his Oakland, California bar. I not sure of the name's origins—but maybe it refers to a close encounter with the real thing.

Pour all ingredients into a shaker with ice. Shake sharply. Strain into a glass filled with dry crushed ice. Squeeze a wedge of lime directly in the drink and then drop it in. Serve with a straw.

METHOD: shake
GLASS: highball

1oz/3cl dark rum
½oz/1.5cl white rum
½oz/1.5cl brandy
⅓oz/1cl triple sec or Cointreau
1¾oz/5cl freshly squeezed orange juice
juice of half a lime

SCREWDRIVER

Created in the 1950s when an American oil man based in Iran allegedly stirred this combination with a screwdriver. I like to make it quickly with fresh orange juice to bring out the full flavor.

Pour the vodka into a glass. Add orange juice and stir. Garnish with a slice of orange. Serve with a stirrer.

METHOD: build
GLASS: highball

1¾oz/5cl vodka
5oz/15cl freshly squeezed orange juice

SEA BREEZE

METHOD: build
GLASS: highball

1¾oz/5cl vodka
3½oz/10cl cranberry
  juice
1¾oz/5cl fresh
  grapefruit juice

In the 1930s, a Sea Breeze was made of gin, apricot brandy, grenadine, and lemon juice. Later recipes featured vodka, dry vermouth, Galliano, and Blue Curaçao. But this combination of vodka, cranberry, and grapefruit juices is considered the modern classic.

Pour the ingredients into a glass filled with ice. Stir. Garnish with a wedge of lime. Serve with a stirrer.

SEX ON THE BEACH

METHOD: shake
GLASS: highball

1oz/3cl vodka
½oz/1.5cl peach
  schnapps
½oz/1.5cl Chambord
1¾oz/5cl freshly
  squeezed orange
  juice
1¾oz/5cl cranberry
  juice

This popular version is made with vodka, peach schnapps, Chambord, and orange and cranberry juices. Some recipes have used raspberry liqueur, melon liqueur, and vodka, and pineapple and cranberry juices.

Pour all the ingredients in a shaker with ice. Shake sharply. Strain into a glass filled with ice. Garnish with a slice of lime. Serve with a straw and a stirrer.

NB: this drink can be built straight into a glass if you do not want to shake it.

Opposite
Absolut: vodka as art.

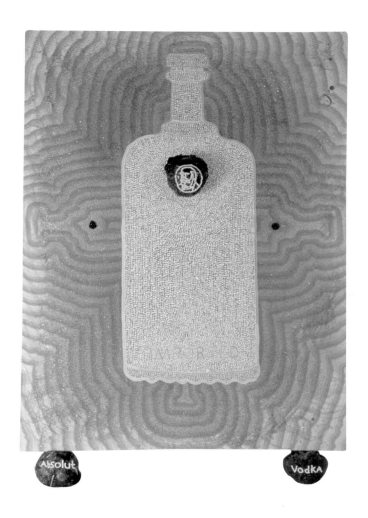

SILVER SUNSET

METHOD: shake
GLASS: highball

1oz/3cl vodka
½oz/1.5cl apricot
brandy
½oz/1.5cl Campari
3oz/9cl fresh orange
juice
½oz/1.5cl lemon juice
1 dash egg white

This drink has been in existence for a while and retains its popularity. The egg white helps to combine the ingredients and gives the drink a head.

Pour all ingredients into a shaker with ice. Shake sharply. Strain into a glass filled with ice. Garnish with a slice of orange and a maraschino cherry. Serve with a straw.

SINGAPORE SLING

A sling can be traced back to 1759 and its name is possibly derived from the German word *schlingen*, meaning "to swallow quickly." Its origin is uncertain and there may be a connection to the Collins.

This original recipe is refreshing. I believe that the Singapore Gin Sling was created at the Raffles Hotel in Singapore in 1915 by bartender Ngiam Tong Boon. By 1930, when the name Singapore Sling arrived in Europe and America, it had lost its fruit juices and was distilled down to gin, cherry brandy, fresh lemon juice, and soda water.

RAFFLES SINGAPORE SLING

Pour all ingredients into a shaker with ice. Shake sharply. Strain into a glass with ice. Garnish with a slice of pineapple and a maraschino cherry. Serve with a straw and a stirrer.

METHOD: shake
GLASS: highball

⅔oz/2cl gin
⅔oz/2cl cherry brandy
⅓oz/1cl Cointreau
⅓oz/1cl Benedictine
⅓oz/1cl fresh lime juice
2½oz/7cl fresh orange juice
2½oz/7cl pineapple juice

SINGAPORE SLING

Place all ingredients, except the soda water, into a shaker with ice. Shake sharply. Strain into a glass. Top up with soda water. Stir. Garnish with a slice of lemon and a maraschino cherry.

METHOD: shake
GLASS: highball

1½oz/4cl gin
⅔oz/2cl cherry brandy
⅔oz/2cl fresh lemon juice
soda water

SLOE GIN FIZZ

METHOD: shake
GLASS: highball

1¾oz/5cl sloe gin
juice of half a lemon
dash gomme syrup
soda water

The original Fizz was mentioned in magazine articles way back in the 1870s, and is another relative of the Collins, the difference being that the Fizz is always shaken.

Many bartenders add egg white to give the cocktail a fizzy head—most impressive. I love the plum flavor that comes to the surface when you mix it with lemon juice and soda water.

Pour all ingredients, except the soda water, into a shaker with ice. Shake sharply. Strain into a glass and fill up with soda water. Garnish with a slice of lime. Serve with a stirrer.

SLOW-HAND LOVER

METHOD: blender
GLASS: colada

1oz/3cl tequila
⅔oz/2cl dark rum
⅓oz/1cl Tia Maria
⅔oz/2cl coconut cream
half a fresh banana
⅓oz/1cl pineapple juice

★ A heady mix of tequila and dark rum, plus the creamy texture of banana and coconut cream, makes this a sensual sip.

Pour all ingredients, except for the rum, into a blender with a scoop of crushed ice. Blend for 15 seconds. Pour into a chilled glass. Float the rum on top. Garnish with a Cape gooseberry. Serve with a straw.

SOUTH PACIFIC

This creation by Gary Revell won best drink in the Australian National Cocktail Competition in the 1980s, and his combination has withstood the onslaught of time.

Pour the gin and Galliano into a glass filled with ice. Stir. Add Seven-Up to almost three-quarters full. Pour the Blue Curaçao gently into the drink and let it sink to the bottom of the glass. Then place a barspoon into the glass, touching the bottom of the glass. Twist it just enough to disturb the Curaçao, which will gently rise and merge with the Galliano. Garnish with a slice of lime on the rim of the glass. Serve with a straw.

METHOD: build
GLASS: highball

1oz/3cl gin
½oz/1.5cl Galliano
½oz/1.5cl Blue Curaçao
Seven-Up

SUMMER LOVE

Pisang Ambon is a delicious green liqueur based on an old Indonesian recipe of exotic herbs and fruits.

Place the vodka, Pisang, limoncello, and lemon juice into a shaker with ice. Shake sharply. Strain into a glass filled with ice. Top up with bitter lemon. Add a stirrer and serve with a clear straw. Garnish with a star fruit.

METHOD: shake/build
GLASS: highball

1oz/3cl Absolut citron vodka
½oz/1½cl Pisang Ambon liqueur
½oz/1½cl limoncello
juice of half a lemon
bitter lemon

SUNNY DREAM

The best cocktail for those who like to add ice cream to a drink. The result is a real smoothie with an apricot/vanilla flavor.

Put the ice cream into the blender and add the remaining ingredients into a blender with half a scoop of dry crushed ice. Blend until smooth. Garnish with a maraschino cherry and a sprig of mint. Serve with a straw.

METHOD: blend
GLASS: goblet

1½oz/4cl apricot brandy
⅔oz/2cl Cointreau
1¾oz/5cl freshly squeezed orange juice
2 tablespoons vanilla ice cream

SWEETHEART

★ Here's a long and refreshing summer aperitif with a delicate hint of bitter orange and sweet lemon.

Put all ingredients into a shaker with ice. Shake quickly. Strain into a glass filled with ice. Garnish with a stem of cranberries on the rim of the glass.

METHOD: shake
GLASS: highball

1oz/3cl vodka
1½oz/4cl Aperol
⅔oz/2cl limoncello
⅔oz/2cl freshly squeezed lemon juice
3½oz/10cl cranberry juice

Opposite
Summer Love (left) and Sweetheart (right).

TEQUILA MOCKINGBIRD

A delicious drink with the strength of the tequila combined with the freshness of crème de menthe and the sharpness of the lime.

Pour all ingredients into a glass filled with crushed ice and fill up with soda water. Stir. Garnish with a sprig of mint set in a wedge of lime. Serve with a straw.

METHOD: build
GLASS: highball

1½oz/4cl silver tequila
⅔oz/2cl green crème de menthe
juice of half a lime

TEQUILA SUNRISE

A 1930s Mexican classic, this is a colorful, long drink to be enjoyed any time of the day.

Pour the tequila and orange juice into a glass with ice and stir. Slowly drop the grenadine into the center and watch it sink to the bottom, creating a sunrise effect. Garnish with a slice of orange and a maraschino cherry. Serve with a straw and a stirrer.

METHOD: build
GLASS: highball

1¾oz/5cl tequila
1 to 2 dashes grenadine
5oz/15cl freshly squeezed orange juice

Opposite
Vampiro (left) and Tequila Sunrise (right).

TROPICAL DAWN

METHOD: shake
GLASS: old-fashioned

1oz/3cl gin
⅔oz/2cl Campari
1¾oz/5cl freshly
    squeezed orange
    juice

A popular cocktail that takes the Campari and orange (the Garibaldi) one step further.

Place all ingredients into a shaker with ice. Shake sharply. Strain into a glass filled with crushed ice. Garnish with a slice of orange and a cherry. Serve with a straw.

VAMPIRO

METHOD: shake
GLASS: highball

1¾oz/5cl silver tequila
2½oz/7cl tomato juice
1oz/3cl orange juice
1 teaspoon clear honey
juice of half a lime
½ slice of onion, finely
    chopped
few thin slices of fresh
    red hot chili
few drops of
    Worcestershire sauce
salt to taste

Opposite
Many early images were artwork, not photographs.

This is the national drink of Mexico, strong and magical. The amount of chili will, of course, depend upon personal taste: the more slices, the hotter the drink. It's a strange combination of orange and tomato juice, all the spices, the sweetness of the honey, and the surprise of onion. It is a truly great drink, as energetic as the salsa!

Pour all ingredients into a shaker with ice. Shake well to enable the flavor of the chili to be released into the liquid. Strain into a glass filled with ice. Garnish with a wedge of lime and a chili (green or red) for anyone devilish enough to dare to take a bite of it!

VELVET ROSA

★ This is named after my mother in Maori and it reflects her bubbly, gentle, and loving nature. A great party drink, or to have with the person you love.

Put all ingredients, except the champagne, into a cocktail shaker with ice. Shake quickly. Strain into a chilled glass and fill up with champagne. Stir quickly to bring the effervescence into play. Garnish with a small, delicate red rose petal.

METHOD: shake/build
GLASS: flute

⅔oz/2cl white rum
⅓oz/1cl peach
   schnapps
1oz/3cl cranberry juice
champagne

WOO-WOO

A weird and wonderfully named drink that reached the height of its popularity in the 1980s, when peach schnapps was flavor of the decade. Formerly known as a Teeny-Weeny Woo-Woo.

Pour all ingredients into a shaker with ice. Shake sharply. Strain into a glass filled with ice. Garnish with a wedge of lime dropped in the drink. Serve with a stirrer.

METHOD: shake
GLASS: old-fashioned

1oz/3cl vodka
⅔oz/2cl peach
   schnapps
1¾oz/5cl cranberry
   juice

Opposite
Maori Magic (left)and Velvet Rosa (right).

ZOMBIE

METHOD: shake
GLASS: highball

½oz/1.5cl white rum
½oz/1.5cl golden rum
½oz/1.5cl dark rum
⅓oz/1cl apricot brandy
dash gomme syrup (or
   1 teaspoon superfine
   sugar)
⅓oz/1cl 151 proof
   Demarara rum
1¾oz/5cl freshly
   squeezed orange
   juice
1¾oz/5cl pineapple
   juice

There will always be debate on the origins of this cocktail, although there is a record of the recipe dating back to 1935. One 1930s story involves Don Beach (formerly known as Ernest Raymond Beaumont-Gannt) of Hollywood's Don the Beachcomber who allegedly created the drink to cure a guest's hangover. When asked if he liked the drink, the customer claimed it had turned him into a zombie.

The second involves Christopher Clark, who had returned from Cap Haitian with the recipe. The third historical mention of the drink can be found in a report of it being served at the 1939 World's Fair in Flushing, New York.

The ingredients, too, can differ. Some call for cherry brandy, others drop it; some call for papaya fruit juice but this is the recipe most commonly regarded as the classic.

Opposite
The allure of the sun and exotic locations provided was used in 1925 to lure people to take vacations on luxury cruise liners.

Pour all ingredients, except the 151° proof Demarara rum, into a shaker with ice. Shake sharply. Strain into a glass filled with dry crushed ice. Carefully float the rum on top. Garnish with a slice of orange and lime and a sprig of mint. Serve with a straw.

NONALCOHOLIC DRINKS

The secret of making a delicious nonalcoholic drink is in being able to disguise the fact that the drink has no alcohol, yet still making it sexy. The combination of juices still gives you the sharp, sweet, and spicy flavors that excite your palate. The various textures combine to make it look good as well. It doesn't disappoint you, it still teases your taste buds. This is the art of the cocktail creator, be the drink with or without alcohol.

There's so much freshness in these drinks, with raspberries, strawberries, blueberries, and cranberries, each alive with rich color and flavor, particularly the citrus varieties. The juices made from them contain the individual fragrances; the nose is so intense that it heightens all of your senses.

Each of these recipes—apart from the Sangrita—is a recipe that I have created during some of the summer holidays I have taken with my family, whether at the beach in Maiori, Italy, or in my bar at home, when we have friends over. These drinks ensure that our friends can drive home safely with their children. I have also re-created many of these in the hotel bar at the end of a long, hot summer's day when guests have wearily asked me for something refreshing, tasty but with no wine or spirits.

The number of fresh or long-life juices available today, either in a carton or a bottle, and the fact that nearly everyone has a blender and/or a juicer in the kitchen make the non-alcoholic drink an easy option. These days, there is also more emphasis on looking and feeling healthy, and drinking exotic combinations of fresh fruit juices is a great way to achieve this new lease of energy. Once you learn about the vitamin content—either A, B, C, D, or E—of each fruit you can learn how to combine them to give you the essential daily vitamins you need to carry on your hectic lifestyle. Specific fruits have a secret energizing content and when you combine these, you can create powerful potions.

There is just as much pleasure in creating a nonalcoholic drink as there is in creating one with a spirit—and you can personalize them by adding or subtracting ingredients.

Following are 15 recipes using either fresh fruit juices or juices from a carton. Have fun with these and remember to add a fancy straw!

TWO TIPS

When I say fill the glass, I mean fill to three-quarters full, leaving space for the mixer.

Always fill the glass with ice cubes unless otherwise stated.

ALLEGRIA

METHOD: blend
GLASS: goblet

half a ripe mango,
    peeled, cut and diced
1¾ oz/5cl carrot juice
1¾ oz/5cl pineapple
    juice
1¾ oz/5cl orange juice
⅔oz/2cl lemon juice
still mineral water

★ The name means "happiness" in Italian. This drink is fresh and healthy—and only 78 calories. That's why it's called happiness!

Put the mango pieces in the blender, add the other ingredients, then a scoop of ice cubes, and blend for 10–15 seconds. Using the lid to stop the ice tumbling into the glass, pour the mixture into a glass filled with fresh ice. Fill almost to the top and then add the still water to dilute the mixture a little. Stir. Garnish with a slice of orange and a maraschino cherry. Serve with a straw.

COCONUT GROVE

METHOD: blend
GLASS: colada

3½oz/10cl pineapple
    juice
1¾oz/5cl coconut cream
1¾oz/5cl fresh pink
    grapefruit juice

★ If I had been a bartender at the renowned nightclub during singer Frank Sinatra's reign, I would have created this delicious mixture for him.

Place ingredients into a blender with a scoop of crushed ice. Blend for 10 seconds and pour directly into a glass. Garnish with a thin segment of grapefruit and a spiral of orange peel. Serve with a straw.

CRACKER

★ So-called because it is a cracker! This is simple to make and delicious to sip on a balmy evening.

Fill a glass with ice. Add the pineapple and passionfruit juices, then pour in the cranberry juice. Finally, add the grapefruit juice, creating a density of both color and flavors. Fill the drink up with Seven-Up and stir. Garnish with a slice of lime. Serve with a straw and a stirrer.

METHOD: build
GLASS: highball

1¾oz/5cl cranberry juice
1¾oz/5cl pineapple juice
1¾oz/5cl passionfruit juice
1¾oz/5cl grapefruit juice
Seven-Up

CRANBERRY FIZZ

★ This is a perfect drink to share with your friends at a summertime party. It's easy to make and looks great in the punch bowl.

Pour all the ingredients, except the Seven-Up, into the punch bowl and place in the refrigerator for a couple of hours before the party begins. Take it out and add the garnishes—thin, triangular slices of pineapple, a stem of cranberries, and thin slices of apple. Place a small sprig of fresh mint in the middle of the bowl. Add ice and Seven-Up when the first guests arrive so that the latter doesn't lose its fizz. Stir.

METHOD: build
GLASS: wine/punch

Serves 12

2 pints/1 litre cranberry juice
2 pints/1 litre clear apple juice
2 pints/1 litre pineapple juice
Seven-Up

FOREST FIZZ

METHOD: blend
GLASS: highball

handful fresh
    blueberries
handful fresh
    blackberries
small handful
    raspberries
⅓oz/1cl freshly
    squeezed lemon juice
1 teaspoon
    superfine sugar
5oz/15cl soda water

Opposite
Forest Fizz (left) and
White Sandy Beach
(right).

★ Imagine the leafy canopy of young trees, imagine the juices oozing from these three berries and you almost have the picture of what this drink tastes like.

Place the berries in a blender with the lemon juice. Sprinkle the sugar over the berries. Blend until smooth. Strain the purée mixture through a nylon strainer or a fine cheesecloth into a glass filled with ice. Top it up with soda water. Stir.(If you can, use blueberry soda to give the best flavor.) Garnish with a selection of berries on a toothpick across the drink, and a sprig of mint on top in the middle. Serve with a straw.

GINGER ALERT

METHOD: shaker
GLASS: highball

3½oz/10cl clear apple
    juice
1¾oz/5cl clear pear
    juice
⅔oz/2cl lemon juice
small piece gingerroot
ginger ale

★ A drink designed to give your system a wake-up call, it is a great fusion of juice and ginger flavor.

Put the apple, pear, and lemon juices into a shaker with ice. Grate the ginger into the shaker. Shake to let the juices soak up the ginger flavor. Strain into a glass with ice. Top up with ginger ale. Stir. Garnish with a wedge of apple. Serve with a straw.

ISLAND SURFER

METHOD: blend
GLASS: large goblet

2¾oz/8cl fresh
  mandarin juice
1½oz/4cl pineapple
  juice
1 kiwifruit, peeled and
  diced
4 strawberries, diced

★ The combination of these two colorful fruits and juices produces a smooth, textured drink full of flavor, with the mandarin dominating.

Put all ingredients into the blender and blend until smooth. Add a scoop of crushed ice and blend briefly. Then pour into a glass. Garnish with a slice of kiwifruit. Serve with a straw.

KIWI PUNCH

METHOD: blend/build
GLASS: wine glass

Serves 10

12 kiwifruit
2 bottles alcohol-free
  wine
1 teaspoon sugar
1¾oz/5cl kiwi syrup
juice of 2 lemons
2 pints/1 litre Seven-Up

Opposite
*Cracker (left) and
Kiwi Punch (right).*

★ A little beauty from the southern hemisphere with a gorgeous green hue that will remind all Kiwis of the land of the long white cloud.

Peel and blend the kiwifruit and drain through cheesecloth or a strainer to collect the juice. Or, use an electric juicer if you have one, then you will not need to strain the fruit purée. Add the syrup. Pour the alcohol-free wine into a punch bowl and mix in the kiwifruit and syrup mixture. Add the Seven-Up.
    Garnish with a few slices of peeled kiwifruit and small strawberries afloat in the punch. Use soda water if you prefer a drier taste.

164

MAGIC MOMENT

METHOD: build
GLASS: highball

3½oz/10cl red or white
    grape juice
juice of half a lemon
⅔oz/2cl strawberry
    syrup
soda water

★ You really want to catch the moment these ingredients come together for a full burst of flavor. It's very simple to make. I prefer to use a white grape juice, since it creates a soft contrast against the deep pink of the strawberry syrup.

Pour all ingredients, except soda water, directly into a glass filled with ice. Top it up with soda water and stir. Garnish with a few grapes sitting on the rim of the glass. Serve with a straw.

MY MINT TEA

METHOD: build
GLASS: highball

Serves 2

A bunch of fresh mint
2 pints/1 litre boiling
    water
juice of 1 lemon
1 teaspoon
    lavender honey

★ My wife, Sue, likes to drink this sitting in the garden room on a hot afternoon, with her two boxer dogs at her feet. This is a very good *digestif*, soothing to the stomach.

Put the mint leaves in a heatproof jug and pour the boiling water over. Add the honey and lemon juice and stir to let the ingredients infuse. Leave to cool. When cool, remove the mint leaves. Pour into 2 glasses filled with ice. Add a small sprig of fresh mint and a slice of lime. Serve.

ON THE BEACH

★ Where else do you go on a summer's day and how to quench your thirst?

Pour all ingredients, except the Seven-Up, into a blender. Blend without ice, then add a scoop of ice. Blend for 10 seconds more. Pour into a glass filled with ice and fill up with Seven-Up. Stir. Garnish with tiny melon balls and raspberries skewered on a toothpick placed across the glass. Serve with a straw.

METHOD: blend
GLASS: large goblet

3½oz /100g diced ripe yellow melon
3½oz /100g raspberries
3½oz/10cl freshly squeezed orange juice
dash grenadine
⅓oz/1cl fresh lime juice
Seven-Up

SANGRITA

This is a traditional Mexican drink that wakes up your taste buds. I like the citrus flavor and the hint of the raw onion (maybe because I am Italian!). Prepare at least 2 hours before you need to serve it at a party.

Pour all ingredients into a mixing bowl. Stir well, to make sure the honey is dissolved. Place in the refrigerator to chill for about 2 hours, then strain into a large glass jug. Serve from the jug.

METHOD: build
GLASS: short tumbler

Serves 10 people

2 pints/1 litre tomato juice
17½oz/50cl orange juice
5 teaspoons clear honey
juice of 3 limes
pinch table salt
1 chilli, finely chopped
1 tablespoon finely chopped white onion
ground pepper
10 to 20 drops Worcestershire sauce

SENSATION

METHOD: shake
GLASS: highball

3½ oz/10cl tomato juice
1¾oz/5cl passionfruit
   juice
1¾oz/5cl carrot juice
½oz/1cl lemon juice
1 teaspoon clear honey
3 to 4 dashes
   Worcestershire sauce

★ The perfect combination of sharp, sweet, and spicy flavors to create a taste sensation. Naughty but nice on a summer's night.

Pour all the ingredients into a shaker filled with ice. Shake vigorously to dissolve the honey. Pour the mixture into a glass filled with ice. Garnish with a cherry tomato and a sprig of basil as a stalk. The freshness of the basil makes this a very enlivening drink.

SUMMER SUNSET

★ A refreshing a drink full of vitamins and energy—the papaya contains medicinal qualities—to take you you through the day, whatever you may be doing. It has an impressive red and yellow glow. If preparing a day in advance, do not add the ice until you are ready to serve it.

Scoop out the seeds from the fruit and discard. Dice the flesh of the fruit ready for the blender. Put the fruit into a blender and add the passionfruit and peach juices. Add a squeeze of the lemon and a few drops of grenadine. Blend for 15 seconds to let the fruit combine well with the juice. Then add 2 scoops of ice cubes and blend 10 seconds longer to chill the drink. Fill 4 glasses with ice and pour in the liquid to three-quarters full. The drinks will be pale red. The final touch: float the freshly squeezed orange juice over the top of each: the orange will sit on top of the juices, and gradually drizzle its way in fine strands to the bottom of the glasses. Garnish each drink with a small sprig of fresh mint set in the center of a strawberry. Serve with a straw.

METHOD: blend
GLASS: highball

Serves 4

half a yellow melon
half a papaya
half a mango
6 strawberries
7oz/20cl half a pint
    passionfruit juice
7oz/20cl half a pint
    peach juice
grenadine
1 lemon
freshly squeezed juice
    of 1 orange

Opposite
Lemons growing in a courtyard of Bar Pineta in Maiori, Italy.

WHITE SANDY BEACH

METHOD: blend
GLASS: colada

3½oz/10cl pineapple
  juice
1¾oz/5cl coconut cream
1 small ripe banana

★ This cocktail was created in Little Dick's Bay in the British Virgin Islands, which has a beautiful fine white sandy beach. Paradise! This drink has a wonderful combination of a colada with a banana texture. It's refreshing, and the color of a stretch of white sand.

Place all ingredients into a blender with a scoop of crushed ice. Blend for 15 seconds until smooth and pour the mixture into a chilled glass. Garnish with 3 slices of banana on a toothpick placed across the glass. Add a sprinkle of nutmeg to finish the drink. Serve with a straw.

Opposite
*A Malibu girl conjures up
an exotic cocktail world.*

INDEX

Page 60 (left) *St Hubert* water glass and (right) *Barsac* coupe, both Lalique; Page 63: (left) classic cocktail glass, Dartington and (right) Crackleglass cocktail glass, Nick Munro; Page 68:Silverfish glass tray with pewter rim and hand-applied sterling silver fish pattern, Nick Munro, with *Louvre* cocktail glass, Lalique ; Page 76: (left) *Earth Star* tumbler by Louise Kennedy, Thomas Goode, London, and (right) *Aura* tumbler by Jasper Conran, Waterford Crystal; Page 80: *La Fenice* handblown wine glass from Murano, Selfridges & Co, London; Page 87: *Ice* double cocktail glass by Jasper Conran, Waterford Crystal; Page 93: (left) *Eternity* goblet by Dartington Crystal and (right) *Highlands*, Lalique; Page 96: (left) *Eternity* flute, Dartington Crystal and (right) *Cluny* martini glass, Christofle; Page 106: (left) *Eternity* tall and tumbler, Dartington Crystal; Page 111: *Clos Vougeot* water glass, Lalique; Page 116: Royales de Champagnes wine glass, Thomas Goode; Page 121: (left) *Spindle Tree* tumbler and highball by Louise Kennedy, Thomas Goode; Page 123: *Rachael* jug, Dartington Crystal and Murano glass with hand-painted fish, Harrods; Page 125: (left) *Bubble* tumbler by Saint-Louis, Selfridges & Co and (right) *Roberta* martini glass, Thomas Goode; Page 132: (left) *Langeais* water glass No. 1, Lalique and (right) tumbler by Nason & Moretti of Murano, Selfridges & Co; Page 148: (left) *Vendome* red wine glass and (right) *Louvre* beer glass, Lalique; Page 150: (left) *Geo* tumbler by John Rochas, Waterford Crystal and Saint-Louis *Cosmos* platinum highball glass, Thomas Goode; Page154: (left) *Millenium* flute, Lalique and (right) Carlo Moretti of Murano handmade flute, Thomas Goode; Page 163: (left) *Aida* wine glass by Royal Copenhagen, Selfridges & Co and tumbler by Nason & Moretti of Murano (left), Thomas Goode; Page 165: *Rachael* water glass, Dartington Crystal and (right) *Convesso* by Vilca, Selfridges & Co.

Picture credits: Front cover: James Duncan, back cover: UDV; p.6, Tattinger Champagne; pp.10, 27, 29, 31, 51, 72, 95, 127, 131, 171, UDV Archives; p.14, Bols, Holland; p.16, 39, 47, 65, 136/7, 157, The Advertising Archive; p.20, Waring Blenders, USA; pp.24, 26, 54, 56, 64, 67, Vin Mag Archive Ltd, London; p.34, 143, Absolut, p.36/7, Ketel One Vodka, Holland; p.42, 49, 115, Bacardi; p.58, South American Pictures, UK; p.75, 100, Campari; p.81, E.DE.RA., Italy; p.83, 153, Moet & Chandon; p.117, Cointreau.